COMPASSION
MINISTRIES

Biblical Foundations
Practical Applications

PERRY HANCOCK, PHD

Dedication

This book is dedicated to those who have compassion in their hearts for people, to those who are willing to do church differently in order to reach people with the love of God and the good news of Jesus Christ, to those who are meeting needs and changing lives in Jesus' name, to my dear wife who loves the ladies she serves, and to my mother and sister who loved people with the love of the Lord.

A Word from the Author

Of the five purposes of the church, service has always been a passion of mine. I love worship, both corporate and private. Discipleship is so important in growing believers. Fellowship makes us part of a family which everyone needs. Sharing the good news, evangelism, is our great commission from God. But service has always been a focus of my work.

Two lifetimes ago, as a pastor, I found myself preaching about service on a regular basis. I proclaimed the truth that going to church was to help us be the church in the world. I taught them that ministry evangelism was one of the best ways to reach people for Christ. I shared all those challenges and many others. But, for the most part, I did not lead those churches to have a compassion ministry orientation.

After a decade of pastoring, I began teaching at New Orleans Baptist Theological Seminary. Midway through my tenure at NOBTS I became personally involved in compassion ministries. It was through those experiences that I was emboldened to begin sharing with my students and others the importance and effectiveness of compassion ministry. Eventually, that focus changed the direction of my own ministry.

The single purpose of this book is to provide a resource for local churches and other Christian ministries that will lead to needs met and lives changed by the power of the gospel. May God bless you and use your compassionate heart to lead people to Jesus.

Introduction

This book presents biblical foundations and practical applications for service-based ministries in Christian churches and other Christian organizations. It provides a clear framework for developing effective compassion ministries that meet needs and change lives.

The biblical study begins with a discussion of compassion in Genesis. This chapter highlights how God's compassionate nature is revealed in the creation narrative. There is a focus on the goodness of God and His compassionate acts of kindness and support.

The following chapter focuses on the compassionate heart of God showing that compassion is an essential element of His being and character. The next chapter focuses on compassion in the Old Testament. Discussions include thoughts on compassion as illustrated in Exodus, the Psalms, Wisdom Literature, and the writings of the Prophets.

The next chapter provides a detailed and intimate look at the compassionate heart of Jesus. A study of compassion in the New Testament follows and examines how compassion is an essential virtue for followers of Jesus. From the Gospels to the Epistles, compassion is featured as a dominant theme in the early church.

The book transitions to the provision of practical applications supported by the biblical principles discovered in the earlier chapters. Coverage begins with a look at how Christians can cultivate a compassionate heart. This chapter helps readers develop a personal disposition toward compassion, reflecting the transformative love of Jesus Christ in both word and deed.

In the following chapter, the CARE Ministry Model is presented. CARE is a practical framework for implementing compassionate ministries within the church. The four components are both interrelated and progressive.

The next chapter provides strategies for the creation of a compassionate culture in the local church. A culture of compassion within a church is essential for fostering a community that reflects the love and grace of Christ.

To implement effective compassion ministries churches must adopt strategies that are both intentional and sustainable. Chapter 9 explores three key components for implementing compassion ministries: assessing church ministry capacity, assessing community needs, and strategic planning.

Evangelism and compassion are two vital aspects of Christian ministry that, when combined, create a powerful and holistic approach to sharing the gospel. This last chapter looks at the relationship between the two.

Additional resources are also provided. They include compassion-focused books, an insightful article on generational poverty, a church ministry inventory guide, a community needs survey guide, and information about the author.

This purpose of this book is to inspire you and equip you to serve others and share the good news in Jesus' name. Welcome to *Compassion Ministries: Biblical Foundations – Practical Applications.*

Table of Contents

PART 1

1 The Genesis Of Compassion................................13

2 The Compassionate Heart of God 21

3 Compassion In The Old Testament...................35

4 The Compassionate Heart of Jesus...................52

5 Compassion In The New Testament.................67

6 The Role Of The Holy Spirit................................86

PART 2

7 Cultivating A Compassionate Heart.................91

8 The CARE Ministry Model 112

9 Creating a Culture of Compassion 121

10 Church and Community Assessment................127

11 Evangelism and Compassion Ministry................. 135

Chapter Sources
Additional Resources
Article – Generational Poverty
Church Ministry Inventory Guide
Community Needs Survey Guide
About The Author, Perry Hancock
Additional Books by Perry Hancock

PART 1
Biblical Foundations

The Lord God planted a garden in Eden
Genesis 2:8

1   *The Genesis of Compassion*

The concept of compassion ministry is intricately woven into the fabric of the creation story. The Genesis account lays the groundwork for understanding the biblical basis for compassion ministry. This chapter explores what it means to be created in God's image and how this compels us to reflect His character in our daily lives.

We will also examine how the Genesis narrative illustrates God's compassionate response to our vulnerability, particularly in the context of creation and the subsequent fall. Furthermore, we will consider the theological significance of compassion as it relates to our identity as image-bearers and our calling to serve others.

By understanding the genesis of compassion through the lens of the creation narrative, we can better appreciate the depth of God's love and the responsibility that comes with being made in His image. This exploration will not only enrich our theological understanding but also inspire us to engage in acts of compassion that reflect the heart of our Creator.

The Goodness of God in Creation

The goodness of God in creation is a central theme in the Bible, beginning with the very first chapters of Genesis. In the opening verses of Genesis 1, we see God's creative power displayed as He speaks the universe into existence. The repeated phrase, "And God saw that it was good," underscores the intrinsic goodness of everything He made. Each aspect of creation—from the light and the sky to the land, seas, vegetation, animals, and humans—reflects God's perfect and benevolent nature. The creation narrative reveals that God's goodness is not only evident in the beauty and order of the world but also in the intentionality and purpose behind everything He made.

Humanity's creation in God's image is perhaps the most profound expression of His goodness in creation. Genesis 1:26-27 tells us that God created man and woman in His image, giving them dominion over the earth and entrusting them with the responsibility to care for it. This act of creation shows that God intended humans to reflect His character, to live in harmony with one another and with the rest of creation, and to enjoy a relationship with Him. The goodness of God is evident in the dignity and value He bestowed upon humanity, setting them apart from the rest of creation as His image-bearers.

The Garden of Eden, described in Genesis 2, further illustrates God's goodness in creation. The garden was a place of abundance, beauty, and perfect harmony, where Adam and Eve could freely enjoy the fruits of God's creation. Every need was provided for, and there was no pain, suffering, or death. The goodness of God is reflected in the way He designed the garden as a place of delight and sustenance, where humanity could thrive in His presence. The garden represents the ideal state of creation, where God's goodness was fully experienced and enjoyed by His creatures.

The story of creation unfolds over six days, each marked by specific acts of creation followed by God's affirmation that what He created is good. The consistent theme of goodness throughout the creation process highlights God's intentionality and care. Each aspect of creation is not merely functional but is imbued with purpose, reflecting the character of a good God who desires a harmonious and flourishing world.

The Image of God

The creation of humanity is a pivotal moment in the Genesis narrative. In Genesis 1:26 God declares, "Let us make mankind in our image, in our likeness." This statement carries significant theological

> *Being made in the image of God carries with it the imperative to reflect His character in our lives.*

implications. Being created in the image of God signifies that humanity shares certain attributes with the Creator, including the capacity for reason, creativity, and moral understanding. The phrase "in our image" suggests a communal aspect of God's nature, hinting at the relational dynamic within the Trinity. This divine likeness calls us to reflect God's character in our interactions with others and the world.

The phrase "image of God" (imago Dei) encompasses various dimensions that reflect God's nature in humanity. Theologically, this concept can be understood through moral, spiritual, and relational lenses.

- **Moral Dimension**: Being created in God's image endows humanity with a moral compass, enabling individuals to discern right from wrong. This moral aspect reflects God's justice and righteousness, as we are called to live according to His ethical standards. The ability to choose between good and evil signifies a responsibility to uphold justice and compassion in our actions.

- **Spiritual Dimension**: The spiritual aspect of the image of God relates to humanity's capacity for relationship with the divine. Unlike the rest of creation, we possess a spiritual essence that allows for communion with God. This connection emphasizes the importance of worship, prayer, and spiritual growth, as individuals seek to deepen their relationship with their Creator.

- **Relational Dimension**: The relational dimension highlights the communal aspect of being made in God's image. Just as God exists in a triune relationship (Father, Son, and Holy Spirit), we are created for relationships with one another. This interconnectedness calls for compassion, empathy, and love in our interactions, reflecting the relational nature of God.

Being made in the image of God carries with it the imperative to reflect His character in our lives. This reflection is particularly evident in the call to embody compassion. Throughout Scripture, God is portrayed as compassionate, merciful, and loving.

As image-bearers, we are called to mirror these attributes in our relationships with others. This includes showing kindness to the vulnerable and extending grace to those in need. Thus, reflecting God's character, particularly His compassion, becomes a central aspect of living out our identity as His followers. His compassion in us becomes visible to everyone we meet.

The doctrine of the imago Dei also has profound implications for human dignity and worth. Since we are all created in the image of God, we possess inherent value and should be treated with respect and dignity. This equality transcends race, gender, nationality, and socio-economic status, affirming that every person is deserving of compassion and justice.

The creation narrative in Genesis presents a God who is not only powerful but also deeply compassionate. From the outset, God's creative acts demonstrate His intention to provide for and care for His creation. God's provision is

> *The creation narrative in Genesis presents a God who is not only powerful but also deeply compassionate.*

evident in the way He creates a suitable environment for humanity. In Genesis 2:8-9, He plants a garden filled with trees that are pleasing to the eye and good for food. This act of generosity illustrates God's desire for humanity to thrive in a nurturing environment.

Throughout the creation narrative, we see multiple examples of God's compassion. One striking instance is found in Genesis 3, following the fall of humanity. The Fall, initiated by Adam and

Eve's disobedience, introduces a significant rupture in the relationship between God and humanity. The serpent's deception leads Eve to eat from the forbidden tree, and Adam follows suit (Genesis 3:6). This act of rebellion against God's command results in immediate consequences, not only for Adam and Eve but for all of creation.

Despite the gravity of their sin, God's response to Adam and Eve reveals His unwavering compassion. After they disobey, God seeks them out, asking, "Where are you?" (Genesis 3:9). This question is not one of condemnation but rather an expression of God's desire to restore the broken relationship. It demonstrates His initiative in seeking reconciliation, even when humanity has turned away from Him.

God's inquiry reflects His compassionate nature, as He does not abandon His creation to the consequences of sin. Instead, He actively engages with Adam and Eve, inviting them to confront their actions. This pursuit highlights the heart of God, who longs for humanity to return to Him, despite their failure. It serves as a reminder that God's compassion is not contingent upon human perfection; rather, it is a steadfast response to human vulnerability and need.

In addition to seeking Adam and Eve, God demonstrates His compassion through the provision of garments to cover their nakedness. After their eyes are opened, they realize their shame and attempt to cover themselves with fig leaves (Genesis 3:7). But God takes it upon Himself to provide garments of skin for them (Genesis 3:21). This act signifies His care and mercy, even in the face of their disobedience.

The provision of garments is symbolic of God's desire to cover human shame and restore dignity. It foreshadows the ultimate act of compassion found in the redemptive work of Christ, who offers forgiveness and restoration to humanity. Just as God clothed Adam and Eve, He provides a way for all of humanity to be clothed in righteousness through faith in Jesus.

Compassion ministry, rooted in the creation story, also reflects God's desire for humanity to care for each other as God cared for Adam and Eve. It calls on us to be involved as His agents of love, care, and restoration. We recognize the struggles of those around us and we respond with empathy and action. Compassion ministry, therefore, is rooted in the understanding that all people experience vulnerability, and it is the responsibility of those who reflect God's image to respond with compassionate support.

So, as we participate in compassion ministry, we fulfill our calling as image-bearers of God, reflecting His love and grace in a world that desperately needs His presence in their lives. In doing so, we not only honor God's original design for creation but also participate in the ongoing work of restoration and healing in the lives of those around us.

I encourage you to become actively engaged in compassion ministry as a reflection of your identity in Christ. Seek opportunities to serve and build relationships within your community. Let your actions be a testament to the compassionate nature of God, demonstrating His love to those who are vulnerable and weak.

As you step into this calling, remember that you are not alone; you are part of a larger movement of believers committed to reflecting God's image and making a meaningful impact in the world. Together, we can bring light and hope to those in need, fulfilling our divine mandate to care for each other.

The Lord is gracious and full of compassion.
Psalm 145:8

2   *The Compassionate Heart of God*

The God of the Bible loves people. Love is an essential element of His being and character. God is love. He cannot be God without love. Is he the God of justice? Yes. Is he the God of truth? Yes. Is he God Almighty? Yes. He is also God whose heart is filled with love and compassion for people.

God's love knows no bounds. He loves the Christian and the non-Christian. He loves the agnostic. He loves the Hindu and the Muslim. He loves the rich and the poor. He loves without regard for race, or any other designation ascribed by man. God loves those who do not love Him. He loves those who oppose him. He loves those who are indifferent toward

> *God's love knows no bounds. He loves without regard for any designation ascribed by man. God loves people.*

him. He loves those who do not believe that He exists. God loves people.

Another essential element of God's character is compassion. Compassion is a result of God's great love. Because God loves, He cares. Scripture reveals God's heart of love and compassion. The Old Testament provides ample evidence for the claim that God is a God of love. Many who have provided Old Testament commentary have neglected to present the loving nature of God. They often limit their discussions to the role of God as the Lawgiver. They major on the wrath and judgment of God. Are those attributes of God real? Yes. Scripture also reveals to us a loving, merciful, and, yes, compassionate God.

In Hebrew, the word *compassion* is found in three basic forms with one having two different expressions. The first use of the word is found in Exodus 2:6. The word is *chamal* which means 'to spare' or 'to have pity'. It is associated with the love of a mother for a child.

> *And when she had opened it, she saw the child: and, behold, the babe wept. And she had compassion on him, and said, This is one of the Hebrews' children.*   Exodus 2:6 KJV

A more specialized form of *compassion* is *racham*. With one exception, *racham* is used to note God's compassion for His people. The word means 'to love deeply' or 'to show mercy'. In the King James Version of the Bible, the most common rendering of *racham* is *mercy*.

And he said, I will make all my goodness pass before thee,
and I will proclaim the name of the LORD before thee; and
will be gracious to whom I will be gracious and will shew
mercy on whom I will shew mercy. Exodus 33:19 KJV

Racham is closely associated with *rechem* which is the Hebrew word for *womb*. Again, the word is related to the love of a mother for her child.

The adjective form of compassion, *compassionate*, is the Hebrew word *rachum*. It is found 13 times in Scripture and refers in all cases to the compassion of God. *Rachum* denotes the fact that compassion is a part of who God is.

But You, Lord, are a compassionate and gracious God, slow
to anger and rich in faithful love and truth. Psalm 86:15

Because compassion is a part of the nature and character of God, His compassion is endless. He cannot and does not withhold His compassion. Even when He disciplines His children, God has compassion on them. God's compassion is also never wavering. There is not a time when He has more or less compassion. His compassion is constant and full.

The LORD'S lovingkindnesses indeed never ceases, For His
compassions never fail. Lamentations 3:22

Compassion is also translated *mercy* or *pity*. Mercy is the most common rendering in the KJV. The dominant Hebrew word for mercy is *hesed*. It refers to God's love toward the people with whom He has a covenant relationship. In the Old Testament,

God's compassion is most often expressed in the relationship He has with His people.

> *As a father has compassion on his children, so the LORD has compassion on those who fear Him.* Psalm 103:13

God's compassion for His covenant people was often expressed in terms of His long suffering for their sins. Throughout Israel's history of disobedience, God's compassion is seen in His forgiveness and the restoration of His relationship with His people. It was God's great compassion that allowed the people to continue their journey with Him. The story of Israel would have ended long ago had it not been for the mercy and compassion of God.

> *...return to the LORD your God. For He is gracious and compassionate, slow to anger, rich in faithful love, and He relents from sending disaster.* Joel 2:13

Compassion, therefore, is a part of who God is. He loves people from the depths of His being. He loves like a parent, with all His heart. His compassion is a love that is likened to mercy. When His children disobey, He is anxious to restore His relationship with them.

Compassion is not only a part of who God is and how God feels, but compassion moves God to action. Grammatically, *compassion* is a noun and *compassionate* is an adjective. In the Old Testament, compassion is most often connected, however, with a verb that leads to this powerful truth. Repeatedly the writers of Scripture declare the fact that God acts on His compassion. God loves.

Because He loves, He cares. Because He cares, He moves. God acts upon His compassion at times by restraining Himself. This omnipotent God chooses not to exercise His power, at times, because of His great compassion.

> *Yet He was compassionate; He atoned for their guilt and did not destroy them. He often turned His anger aside and did not unleash all His wrath.* Psalm 78:38

At other times, God acts on His compassion by providing for His people. Because of His great compassion, God leads and guides. His compassion moves Him to provide for His people. God's compassion causes Him to protect and defend. His compassion also moves Him to forgive. Several times in Nehemiah 9, the writer speaks of God's acts of compassion.

> *But You are a forgiving God, gracious and compassionate, slow to anger, and rich in faithful love, and You did not abandon them.* Nehemiah 9:17

> *You did not abandon them in the wilderness because of Your great compassion. During the day, the pillar of cloud never turned away from them, guiding them on their journey. And during the night the pillar of fire illuminated the way they should go.* Nehemiah 9:19

> *In Your abundant compassion, You gave them deliverers, who rescued them from… their enemies.* Nehemiah 9:27

The heart of God for His covenant people is undeniable. He loves them without failing. But God's love is not limited to those who know Him and follow Him. He has compassion for all.

> *The LORD is good to everyone; His compassion rests on all He has made.* Psalm 145:9

God loves the poor. He loves the orphan. He loves the widow. He loves the stranger. He loves the homeless. He loves the oppressed. He loves those who are suffering. He loves the helpless. He loves the hopeless. They are all the objects of His love and compassion. They are always on His mind and heart. He is forever interested in their welfare.

The Old Testament provides a clear picture of God's heart for those in need. The Psalmist wrote often of God's great compassion for the needy.

> *He will have compassion on the poor and needy, And the lives of the needy He will save.* Psalm 72:3 NASB

> *He raises the poor from the dust and lifts the needy from the garbage pile in order to seat them with nobles — with the nobles of His people.* Psalm 113:7, 8

God's compassion for those in need, again, moves Him to action. God provides for the poor. He shelters those in need. He defends those who are oppressed. His compassion will not allow Him to sit idle while people suffer. He rises and supports the weak.

"Because of the oppression of the afflicted and the groaning of the poor, I will now rise up," says the LORD." I will put the one who longs for it in a safe place." Psalm 12:5

You have been a refuge for the poor, a refuge for the needy in their distress, a shelter from the storm, and a shade from the heat. Isaiah 25:4 NIV

The afflicted and needy are seeking water, but there is none, And their tongue is parched with thirst; I, the LORD, will answer them Myself... Isaiah 41:17

A close study of God's compassion for those in need reveals that God has a particular concern for three distinct groups of people, namely, the widows, orphans, and sojourners. Widows and orphans were among the most vulnerable in society. A woman who did not remarry, normally, had no viable means of support. The orphan had no father. The orphan could be the child of a widow.

> *God has a particular concern for three distinct groups of people, namely, the widows, orphans, and strangers.*

Orphans were even more vulnerable than their mothers. Often, they were relegated to begging to survive. The children became victims of abuse. Many were used in human trafficking and forced to work as slaves.

The sojourner was a stranger or a resident in a land that was not his own. Abraham was a sojourner in Hebron. Moses was a sojourner in Midian. Moses named his son who was born in Midian, Gershom, which is translated, as *a sojourner there.* Those traveling in foreign lands were often subject to ridicule and discrimination. They were among the most disadvantaged of their day. They were vulnerable to abuse and frequently disregarded by society.

These three groups have a special place in God's heart. Scripture reveals that great love.

> *God in His holy dwelling is a father of the fatherless and a champion of widows.* Psalm 68:5

> *He executes justice for the fatherless and the widow, and loves the foreigner, giving him food and clothing.*
> Deuteronomy 10:18

God cares so much for the orphan that He adopts the child who has no father. The widows who have no one to defend them, find in God one who champions their cause. God cares so much for the foreigner that He provides for him the necessities of life.
God's love for the orphan, widow, and sojourner is so strong that He promises judgment on any who would deal with them unjustly.

> *I will come to you in judgment, and I will be ready to witness against... those who oppress the widow and the fatherless... and against those who deny justice to the foreigner. They do not fear Me,"* says the LORD of Hosts.
> Malachi 3:5

God will serve as a witness and as the judge in the case against those who mistreat the widow, orphan, and foreigner. He lets all know that He is watching and that He will pour out His vengeance on those who harm those who are so precious to Him.

God has a heart of compassion for His people and all people. For His compassion to be realized, however, He must have someone who will communicate His great love in word and deed. That is why God commands his

> *...God commands His people to care for those in need. The church is to serve as a bridge...*

people to care for those in need. The church is to serve as a bridge between the heart of God and the objects of his love, namely, anyone in need.

God's command of provision was made, first, concerning those who were a part of the household of faith.

> *If there is a poor person among you, one of your brothers within any of your gates in the land the LORD your God is giving you, you must not be hardhearted or tightfisted toward your poor brother.* Deuteronomy 15:7

God's concern, here, is that His people could be reluctant to help the needy, even those in the family. Rather than simply following His command, God wanted His people to have a desire to give. He is asking for generous hearts which lead to open hands.

This verse in Deuteronomy is preceded by God's command regarding the cancelation of debts every 7 years. If the 7th year was approaching, within a year or so, the people could be tempted not to serve the poor, justifying their lack of action on the fact that soon the poor would find relief. God warns them that His command to help those in need is for all seasons.

> *Be careful that there isn't this wicked thought in your heart,*
> *'The seventh year, the year of canceling debts, is near,' and*
> *you are stingy toward your poor brother and give him*
> *nothing. He will cry out to the* LORD *against you, and you*
> *will be guilty.* Deuteronomy 15:9

With no doubt, God's people are to take care of the poor in the family. But within this passage, God extends His requirement of care to include all who are poor in the land.

> *For the poor will never cease to be in the land; therefore, I*
> *command you, saying, 'You shall freely open your hand to*
> *your brother, to your needy and poor in your land.*
> Deuteronomy 15:11

As God's compassion is for all people, so it should be with the people of God. When needs are seen they should be met with a free and willing heart, expressing the great love of God.

Many of God's commands in the Old Testament regarding the care of the poor are related to the agrarian society in which they lived. The context of those commands may seem foreign to many 21st-century urban and suburban Christians. Some might be tempted to label such commands as obsolete. These passages should be viewed, however, in terms of principles that are not bound by time or setting.

One such command is given in Deuteronomy 24. Those working the olive trees were not to go over the field a second time. The remaining olives were to be left for the stranger, the widow, and the orphan. A related passage is found in the book of Ruth where Naomi and Ruth gleaned corn from the fields of Boaz.

One commandment related to the care of the poor that has a more obvious connection with modern-day Christianity is found in Deuteronomy 14 and 26. God commands His people to take the entire tithe once every three years and give it to the stranger, the Levite, the fatherless, and the widow. The third-year tithe was not to be taken to the place of worship but to storehouses within the community.

> *At the end of every three years, bring a tenth of all your*
> *produce for that year and store it within your gates. Then*
> *the Levite, who has no portion or inheritance among you,*
> *the foreigner, the fatherless, and the widow within your*
> *gates may come, eat, and be satisfied.*
> Deuteronomy 14:28, 29

> *When you have finished paying all the tenth of your*
> *produce in the third year, the year of the tenth, you are to*
> *give it to the Levite, the foreigner, the fatherless, and the*
> *widow, so that they may eat in your towns and be satisfied.*
> Deuteronomy 26:12

Though scholars disagree about the meaning and practice of the third-year tithe, the basic principle is clear. God expects His people to provide care for those in need from the resources that He has provided.

God's commands regarding the care of those in need are not limited to acts of direct aid. God's compassion leads to a concern for the defense of the poor in society. The theme of those commands is justice. The psalmist reveals God's compassion for justice and the poor on several occasions.

> *He will judge Your people with righteousness and Your afflicted ones with justice.* Psalm 72:2

> *The Lord executes acts of righteousness and justice for all the oppressed.* Psalm 103:6

> *I know that the Lord upholds the just cause of the poor, justice for the needy.* Psalm 140:12

Often when God commanded His people to care for those in need, He identified the consequences of disobedience. The stories of those who chose not to provide for the needy are quite telling. Isaiah declared that truth as He witnessed the unjust treatment of the poor in His day.

> *Woe to those enacting crooked statutes and writing oppressive laws to keep the poor from getting a fair trial and to deprive the afflicted among my people of justice so that widows can be their spoil and they can plunder the fatherless. What will you do on the day of punishment when devastation comes from far away? Who will you run to for help? Where will you leave your wealth?* Isaiah 10:1-3

God's compassion for the needy is so strong that He simply cannot let those who would use and abuse the needy go unpunished.

Where God punishes those who neglect or mistreat those in need, He also blesses those who care for the poor. The Old Testament writers proclaimed this promise on several occasions.

A generous person will be blessed, for he shares his food with the poor. Proverbs 22:9

Give generously to the poor, not grudgingly, for the LORD your God will bless you in everything you do. Deuteronomy 15:10 NLT

and if you offer yourself to the hungry, and satisfy the afflicted one, then your light will shine in the darkness, and your night will be like noonday. Isaiah 58:10

One interesting reference to the blessing of God on those who provide for the poor is found in Proverbs 19:17.

Kindness to the poor is a loan to the LORD, and He will give a reward to the lender. Proverbs 19:17

Here, the writer provides this incredible truth: when one helps the poor, God is involved in the transaction. It is as if the act of kindness was done to God who counts it as a loan which He will certainly pay with the interest of blessings.

Throughout the Old Testament, it is clear that God is passionate about the care of the poor. He calls upon His people to provide the care that they need. He accepts no excuses. He makes no exceptions. God holds his people accountable for the care of the stranger, the widow, the orphan, and the rest.

God's ultimate desire is that His people would not only provide care but that they would genuinely care for those in need as He cares for them.

> *The righteous care about justice for the poor, but the wicked have no such concern.* Proverbs 29:7

If God's people would simply follow His command to serve the poor, the needs of the poor would be met. But if His people have the same heart of compassion for the poor that He has, not only will those needs be met but those lives will be changed also.

What then is the heart of God? The heart of God is a compassionate heart that loves people, all people. His compassion moves Him to action. He is particularly passionate about meeting the needs of the widow, the orphan, and the stranger. God's compassion for people runs so deep that He cannot stand injustice. He moves to punish those who would abuse the needy. But He blesses those who serve and bless the poor. God desires that His people would develop the same compassion for those in need that He has. This is the compassionate heart of God.

... blessed is the one who is kind to the needy
Proverbs 14:21

3   Compassion In The Old Testament

Compassion ministry is deeply rooted in the biblical narrative, particularly in the Old Testament, where God's character is revealed through His actions and commands. This chapter will explore the foundations of compassion ministry as demonstrated in the Exodus narrative, the Psalms, Wisdom Literature, and the writings of the Prophets. Each of these texts provides a rich theological framework that underscores the importance of compassion as an essential attribute of God and a fundamental calling for His people.

Compassion In the Pentateuch

Establishing a biblical and theological framework for compassion ministry is essential for understanding how God's character and His expectations for humanity are revealed throughout Scripture. The Pentateuch, comprising the first five books of the Bible,

Genesis, Exodus, Leviticus, Numbers, and Deuteronomy, serves as a foundational text that articulates God's covenant relationship with His people and outlines His divine principles for living in community. Within these texts, compassion emerges as a central theme, reflecting God's heart for justice, mercy, and care for the vulnerable.

Understanding compassion in the context of the Pentateuch is vital for several reasons. First, it provides insight into God's nature as a compassionate Creator who actively responds to human suffering. The narratives

> *God is a compassionate Creator who actively responds to human suffering.*

and laws presented in the Pentateuch illustrate how God not only cares for His people but also calls them to embody that same compassion in their interactions with one another and with anyone in need. This understanding challenges believers to reflect on their own attitudes and actions, encouraging them to engage in compassion ministry as a vital expression of their faith.

Furthermore, the Pentateuch lays the groundwork for the entire biblical narrative, influencing the theological themes that resonate throughout the Old and New Testaments. By examining the principles of compassion found in these texts, we can better appreciate the continuity of God's redemptive plan and the call for His people to act justly and love mercy. This section will explore the significance of compassion within the Pentateuch, highlighting its implications for contemporary ministry and the ongoing relevance of these ancient texts in shaping our understanding of compassion in action.

Compassion in the Exodus narrative is a central theme that reveals God's deep concern for His people, particularly in their time of suffering and oppression. This narrative not only highlights the plight of the Israelites in Egypt but also highlights God's compassionate response through acts of deliverance and provision. By examining the oppression of the Israelites, God's call to Moses, and the acts of compassion during the Exodus, we can gain a deeper understanding of the nature of compassion as it is portrayed in this foundational biblical text.

The story begins with the Israelites living in Egypt, where they initially prospered but eventually became enslaved under a new Pharaoh who feared their growing numbers. In Exodus 1:8-14, the Israelites are subjected to harsh labor and oppression, forced to build cities, and endure brutal treatment. The Pharaoh's decree to kill all male Israelite infants further underscores the severity of their suffering. This illustrates the vulnerability of the Israelites and their desperate need for deliverance.

During this suffering, God remains acutely aware of the plight of His people. Exodus 2:23-25 states that God hears their cries and remembers His covenant with Abraham, Isaac, and Jacob. This acknowledgment of suffering reveals God's compassionate nature; He does not remain distant or indifferent to the pain of His people. Instead, He is emotionally invested in their suffering, demonstrating that compassion involves both awareness and a commitment to act on behalf of those in need.

God's response to the suffering of the Israelites culminates in His call to Moses from the burning bush (Exodus 3:1-10). This encounter is significant as it marks the beginning of God's active intervention in the lives of His people.

During this encounter, God expresses His deep compassion for the Israelites, stating, "I have indeed seen the misery of my people in Egypt. I have heard them crying out because of their slave drivers, and I am concerned about their suffering" (Exodus 3:7). God then commissions Moses to lead the Israelites out of Egypt, demonstrating that compassion often requires human agents to fulfill divine purposes.

After the Israelites leave Egypt, they face new challenges in the wilderness, including hunger and thirst. In Exodus 16, God demonstrated His compassion by providing manna from heaven and quail for food. This

> *God demonstrated His compassion by providing manna from heaven and quail for food.*

miraculous provision underscores God's ongoing care for His people, ensuring that they have what they need to survive.

The provision of manna also serves as a lesson in dependence on God. The Israelites are instructed to gather only what they need for each day, teaching them to trust in God's daily provision. This act of compassion not only addresses their physical needs but also fosters a deeper relationship between God and His people, as they learn to rely on Him for sustenance.

This narrative not only reveals God's character as compassionate and merciful but also serves as a model for how believers are called to respond to the needs of those in their communities. The

Exodus story challenges us to embody compassion, caring for the vulnerable, and reflecting the heart of God in a world that desperately needs His love and grace.

Compassion in the Law, particularly as articulated in Leviticus and Deuteronomy, provides a profound understanding of how God desires His people to live in a relationship with one another and with Him. The laws presented in these books are not mere regulations but are deeply rooted in the character of God, reflecting His great compassion. The discussion covers the Holiness Code and its implications for compassionate living, the Shema, and the call to love, and how these elements form a biblical foundation for compassion ministry.

The Holiness Code found in Leviticus outlines specific laws that emphasize the importance of compassion in community living. In Leviticus 19:9-10, God instructs the Israelites to leave the edges of their fields unharvested and to leave the gleanings of their harvest. These provisions are to be made available for the poor, the widows, and the orphans. This directive reflects God's concern for the vulnerable members of society and establishes a system of care that ensures that no one is left destitute.

By mandating that the community support its most vulnerable members, the Holiness Code emphasizes that compassion is an integral part of living a holy life. The act of leaving food for the poor is not only a practical measure but also a spiritual one, reinforcing the idea that holiness involves active love and care for others. This principle of compassion extends beyond mere charity; it calls for a communal responsibility to uplift those in need.

The command to love one's neighbor as oneself, found in Leviticus 19:18, further reinforces the interconnectedness of love for God and love for others. This principle is foundational to the ethical teachings of the Old Testament and serves as a guiding principle for compassionate living. It challenges individuals to consider the needs and well-being of others as they would their own, fostering a culture of empathy and care. By prioritizing love for one's neighbor, the Israelites are called to create a community that reflects God's compassion, where individuals actively seek the welfare of others and respond to their needs.

Compassion in the Historical Books

Compassion also finds profound expression throughout the historical books of the Old Testament. Here, compassion emerges as a guiding principle in Israel's history, highlighting exemplary figures and narratives that illustrate its transformative power.

Joshua's leadership toward ensuring the protection of Rahab and her family during the fall of Jericho (Joshua 6:22-25) exemplifies compassion transcending cultural boundaries and prevailing over judgment.

Joshua specifically instructs the two spies to rescue Rahab and her family, fulfilling the promise they had made to her earlier. This act of mercy stands out starkly against the backdrop of the city's destruction, highlighting the importance of keeping one's word and showing kindness even in difficult circumstances.

The passage emphasizes that Rahab and her entire household were spared, not just Rahab herself. This extension of compassion to her family members displays a broader understanding of mercy, recognizing the connection between families and communities. It reflects a willingness to save not just an individual, but to preserve an entire family line, demonstrating a more comprehensive and far-reaching form of compassion.

Furthermore, the text notes that Rahab and her family were brought out of the city and placed "outside the camp of Israel." While this might initially seem like exclusion, it represents a thoughtful approach to integration. By giving them a safe place outside the camp, Joshua provided them with protection and a chance to gradually assimilate into Israelite society. This careful handling of Rahab and her family shows compassion not just in sparing their lives, but in considering their long-term welfare.

The era of the Judges and Kings also provides numerous examples of compassionate leadership amidst the tumultuous political landscape of ancient Israel. Judges like Deborah and Samuel combined judicial wisdom with compassion, advocating for justice while addressing the plight of the oppressed.

King David, often revered for his military prowess, also demonstrated compassion, as seen in his care for Mephibosheth, the crippled grandson of Saul. Despite the potential threat Mephibosheth posed as a descendant of the former king, David chose to honor his covenant with Jonathan by seeking out any remaining members of Saul's household to show kindness.

When David learned of Mephibosheth's existence and his disability, he did not hesitate to extend his kindness. This great act of compassion was not just a political gesture but a genuine fulfillment of his promise to Jonathan, showcasing David's loyalty and integrity.

David's compassion is further highlighted by his actions upon meeting Mephibosheth. When Mephibosheth, who had lived in fear and obscurity, was brought before David, he prostrated himself, expecting the worst. Instead, David reassured him, saying, "Don't be afraid, since I intend to show you kindness because of your father Jonathan. I will restore to you all your grandfather Saul's fields, and you will always eat meals at my table." (2 Samuel 9:7). This promise not only alleviated Mephibosheth's fears but also restored his dignity and provided him with a secure and honorable place within the royal household, treating him as one of the king's sons.

David's treatment of Mephibosheth went beyond mere restoration of property; it was an act of profound grace and inclusion. By inviting Mephibosheth to eat at his table continually, David offered him a permanent place of honor and fellowship, symbolizing acceptance, and love. This gesture ensured that Mephibosheth would no longer live in fear or poverty but would enjoy the privileges and protection of the king's household. David's actions serve as a powerful example of compassion, demonstrating how true kindness involves not only meeting immediate needs but also providing ongoing support and inclusion.

Compassion In the Psalms

The Psalms further enrich our understanding of compassion, portraying God as a compassionate protector and caregiver. They express the deep emotional connection between God and humanity, emphasizing His mercy and grace toward those who are vulnerable. The Psalms also refer to the role of God's people in serving as instruments of compassion.

The psalmists frequently praised God for His compassion, describing it as an essential attribute of His character. In Psalm 103:8, David declares, " The LORD is compassionate and gracious, slow to anger and rich in faithful love." This verse highlights the close connection between God's compassion, mercy, and love.

God's compassion is often portrayed as that of a loving father. Psalm 103:13-14 states, " As a father has compassion on his children, so the LORD has compassion for those who fear Him. For He knows what we are made of, remembering that we are dust." This imagery emphasizes God's understanding of human frailty and His tender care for His people.

The psalmists also recognize God's compassion as a source of comfort and hope in times of trouble. In Psalm 86:15-16, David cries out, " But You, Lord, are a compassionate and gracious God, slow to anger and rich in faithful love and truth. Turn to me and be gracious to me. Give Your strength to Your servant; save the son of Your female servant." This passage shows how believers can appeal to God's compassionate nature in their prayers.

The call for compassion on the part of God's people is also presented in the psalms. Psalm 41 offers a vivid portrayal of personal compassion through the lens of caring for the sick and needy. The psalmist speaks of the blessings for those who consider the poor and helpless in Psalm 41:1 (ESV). "Blessed is the one who considers the poor. In the day of trouble, the Lord delivers him." This verse illustrates that compassion is not limited to grand gestures but is often demonstrated best through simple acts of kindness

> *Compassion is not limited to grand gestures but is often demonstrated best through simple acts of kindness.*

toward those in distress. The psalmist emphasizes that caring for the ill and downtrodden reflects divine favor and is a vital aspect of faithful living. The personal nature of compassion as described here suggests that everyone has a role in alleviating suffering, thus making empathy and kindness integral to the communal life of God's people.

The Psalms offer a multifaceted exploration of compassion, emphasizing both divine and human dimensions. Through calls for justice, care for the needy, and reflection on God's merciful nature, these ancient songs encourage believers to practice compassion in their everyday lives.

Compassion In Wisdom Literature

Compassion is also a recurring theme throughout the Wisdom Literature of the Old Testament. These texts provide profound insights into the nature of compassion, its significance in human relationships, and the call to embody compassion in a world marked by suffering and transience. The teachings of Proverbs provide great insight regarding compassion.

The Book of Proverbs emphasizes the importance of compassion in fostering healthy relationships. Proverbs 14:21 states, "... whoever shows kindness to the poor will be happy." This verse highlights the moral imperative to show kindness and compassion, particularly to those who are vulnerable. Compassion is portrayed not only as a virtue but as a reflection of one's character and relationship with God.

Similarly, Proverbs 19:17 declares, " Kindness to the poor is a loan to the LORD, and He will give a reward to the lender." This teaching reinforces the idea that acts of compassion toward the needy are not merely charitable deeds but are seen as service to God Himself. The promise of reward emphasizes that compassion has both earthly and spiritual significance, encouraging individuals to engage in acts of kindness and generosity.

Throughout Proverbs, wisdom is presented as a guiding force that encourages individuals to care for others, especially those in need. The teachings promote a life of compassion and integrity, urging people to support those who are vulnerable. Proverbs 31:8-9 says, "Speak up for those who cannot speak for themselves, for the rights of all who are destitute. Speak up and judge fairly; defend the rights of the poor and needy." This passage emphasizes the importance of standing up for what is right and showing kindness within the community.

The consistent emphasis on caring for those in need reflects the understanding that true wisdom involves recognizing the inherent dignity of all people and responding to their needs. Compassion, therefore, is not just an emotional response but a wise and necessary action that aligns with God's character and intentions for humanity.

Compassion In Prophetic Literature

Compassion in the prophetic literature of the Old Testament emerges as a vital theme that underscores God's concern for those in need. The prophets, as messengers of God, not only called for righteousness but also emphasized the importance of compassion towards those living in poverty.

The writings of the major prophets are replete with references to various aspects of compassion. Jeremiah serves as a rich source of teaching on compassion. In Jeremiah 22:16, the prophet praises King Josiah's compassionate leadership, saying, "He took up the case of the poor and needy, then it went well. Is this not what it means to know Me? This is the LORD's declaration." This verse emphasizes that true knowledge of God is demonstrated through compassionate actions toward the vulnerable in society.

Jeremiah's compassion for the suffering of his people is evident in Jeremiah 8:21-22, where he laments, "For the wound of the daughter of my people is my heart wounded; I mourn, and dismay has taken hold on me. Is there no balm in Gilead? Is there no physician there?" This passage reveals Jeremiah's deep empathy and concern for the afflicted, likening their spiritual condition to a physical ailment in need of healing.

The prophet's commitment to justice and care is further reflected in his critique of those who neglect the needy. In Jeremiah 5:28, he condemns those who do not defend the just cause of the poor. This shows that Jeremiah viewed compassion for the poor and needy as an essential aspect of righteous living.

Jeremiah's ministry also involved advocating for the vulnerable. In Jeremiah 7:5-7, he calls on the people to act justly. "Instead, if you change your ways and your actions, if you act justly toward one

> *Jeremiah's compassion for the needy was integrated into his prophetic message of repentance.*

another, if you no longer oppress the foreigner, the fatherless, and the widow and no longer shed innocent blood in this place or follow other gods, bringing harm on yourselves, I will allow you to live in this place, the land I gave to your ancestors long ago and forever." This passage demonstrates how Jeremiah's compassion for the needy was integrated into his prophetic message of repentance and restoration.

These examples from Jeremiah highlight the prophet's deep concern for the poor and needy, showing how compassion for the vulnerable was central to his understanding of true faith and righteous living.

The book of Ezekiel, while primarily focused on prophecies and visions, does contain references to compassion for the needy. Ezekiel 16:49 addresses the sin of Sodom, stating, "Now this was the sin of your sister Sodom: She and her daughters were arrogant... and unconcerned; they did not help the poor and needy." This verse highlights that neglecting the poor and needy is considered a serious transgression, on par with other sins that led to Sodom's destruction. It implies that showing compassion and helping those in need is a fundamental moral obligation.

The ruin of Sodom came as a result of many sins but among the most grievous was their lack of support for the poor. Once again Ezekiel speaks of these injustices and provides a declaration of judgment and punishment from God.

> *The people of the land have practiced extortion and committed robbery. They have oppressed the poor and needy and unlawfully exploited the foreign residents. So, I have poured out My indignation on them and consumed them with the fire of My fury. I have brought their actions down on their heads." This is the declaration of the Lord GOD.*
> Ezekiel 22:29, 31

In Ezekiel 18:7, the prophet describes the characteristics of a righteous person. "He does not commit robbery but gives his food to the hungry and provides clothing for the naked." This passage emphasizes that compassion for the needy, demonstrated through concrete actions like feeding the hungry and clothing the naked, is an essential aspect of righteous living.

These examples from Ezekiel, while not as numerous as in some other prophetic books, still underscore the importance of compassion for the needy as a fundamental aspect of righteous behavior and good leadership.

The minor prophets also contribute to our understanding of biblical compassion. The main contribution of Amos is a critique of those who abused the poor. One of the most striking passages is Amos 4:1, where the prophet condemns the wealthy women of Samaria who oppressed the poor and crushed the needy. This vivid imagery underscores the severity of their actions and serves as a powerful indictment of those who exploit the vulnerable for their gain. Amos's message here is clear: true faithfulness to God is incompatible with the mistreatment of the poor and needy.

In Micah, we find a memorable question and answer regarding the expectations of the Lord. Micah 6:8 asks. "He has shown you, O mortal, what is good. And what does the Lord require of you? To act justly and to love mercy and to walk humbly with your God." This call to action emphasizes that true worship involves not only ritual practices but also a commitment to justice and compassion in everyday life. The prophets consistently remind the people of Israel that their relationship with God is inextricably linked to their treatment of one another, particularly those in need.

The theological implications of prophetic compassion challenge believers to embody God's heart for justice and mercy in their lives. By responding to the prophetic call to act justly and love mercy, individuals and communities can reflect God's character and contribute to a more compassionate world. The message of the prophets remains relevant today, urging believers to engage in acts of compassion and justice as a vital expression of their faith.

In conclusion, the Old Testament provides a rich theological foundation for compassion, rooted deeply in the very character and actions of God. Throughout its pages, we see a consistent portrayal of Yahweh as a God of mercy, compassion, and loving kindness. This divine compassion is not merely an abstract attribute, but a dynamic force that shapes Israel's history, law, and prophetic vision.

From God's compassionate act of creation to the deliverance of Israel from Egypt, to His patient forgiveness of their repeated transgressions, the narrative of the Old Testament is fundamentally one of divine mercy. The Law, far from being solely punitive, enshrines compassion for the vulnerable as a core ethical imperative. The prophets, even in their harshest judgments, consistently point to God's compassion as the basis for hope and restoration.

This biblical foundation has far-reaching implications. It reveals that compassion is not peripheral to God's nature or His expectations for His people, but central to both. It challenges simplistic notions of the Old Testament God as solely wrathful or judgmental. Instead, it presents a complex portrait of the God whose justice is always tempered by mercy, and whose power is most often expressed through compassion.

Furthermore, there is the presentation of a mandate for God's people. Just as Israel was called to reflect God's character in their communal life and treatment of those in need, so too are we called to embody divine compassion in our own contexts. The Old Testament's emphasis on compassion thus remains profoundly relevant, offering both comfort in God's mercy and a challenging call to extend that mercy to others.

The Old Testament teaching of compassion forms an essential backdrop for understanding God's character, His dealings with humanity, and His expectations for His people. It lays a foundation that the New Testament will build upon, ultimately finding its fullest expression in the compassionate ministry of Jesus Christ.

> *When He saw the crowds, He felt compassion for them…*
> Matthew 9:36

4   *The Compassionate Heart of Jesus*

With a basic New Testament foundation for compassion ministry, we now move to a more detailed and intimate look at the compassionate heart of Jesus. Jesus was God's compassion personified. Compassion dominated His heart, His mind, and His actions. Compassion was not an occasional feeling or thought for Jesus. He was always compassionate. He was never anything less than compassionate. It was a part of the fabric of His being. Jesus was compassion.

Compassion took Jesus everywhere He went. It took Him along the hillsides and along the shores where the common people were. Compassion took Jesus out into the marketplace. It took Him down the back streets and even to the other side of the tracks. Compassion took Jesus to the lowly, the despised, and the outcast.

His compassion was certainly driven by the great spiritual need of mankind. He saw the people as sheep without a shepherd. He knew that without a savior they could never know God. He knew that He was their only hope. It was His compassion that ultimately took Him to the cross to pay for the sins of the world.

Jesus was also compassionate about meeting the here-and-now needs of the people. He was compelled by His compassion to meet the needs of the suffering, the lonely, and the hungry. Repeatedly He heals, feeds,

> *Jesus was compassionate about meeting those here-and-now needs of people. He was truly the Christ of Compassion.*

and meets those kingdom-on-earth needs from His great heart of compassion. Jesus loved people so much that He poured out His compassion on their lives in meaningful and significant ways. He is truly the Christ of Compassion.

In the New Testament, there are six different forms of the word *compassion*. The most common word used for *compassion* is *splagchnizomai*. It occurs first in Matthew 9:36. The basic meaning is 'to be moved deep inside'. The word occurs 17 times in the New Testament. When it is not rendered *compassion* it is rendered *moved*.

> *When He saw the crowds, He felt compassion for them, because they were weary and worn out, like sheep without a shepherd.* Matthew 9:36

Another word used to convey compassion is *eleeo*. It means 'to help the afflicted' or 'to have mercy upon'. It is also used for someone receiving aid or mercy.

> *There were two blind men sitting by the road. When they heard that Jesus was passing by, they cried out, "Lord, have mercy on us, Son of David!"* Matthew 20:30

Two Greek words for compassion appear only once in the New Testament. They are *oikteiro* (Romans 9:15) and *metriopathe*. The first means 'to have pity, a feeling of distress through the ills of others'. The latter is best defined by reading its one occurrence.

> *Who can have compassion on the ignorant, and on them that are out of the way; for that, He also is compassed with infirmity.* Hebrews 5:2 KJV

Two additional Greek words are rendered *compassion*: *sumpatheo*, which is the verb form and *sumpathes* which is the adjective. As the transliteration indicates, the basic meaning of these words is *'sympathy'*. The use of the word in Hebrews 4:15 speaks of the great compassion of Jesus.

> *For we do not have a high priest who is unable to sympathize with our weaknesses, but One who has been tested in every way as we are, yet without sin.*
> Hebrews 4:15

The writer of Hebrews reminded his readers that Jesus understood their struggles and because He knew He had compassion on the people.

> *Jesus left Heaven because of His great love and compassion. He was compassion personified.*

Compassion, for Jesus, was not simply an emotion or a feeling. Compassion for the Savior always meant taking action. Jesus left Heaven because of His great love and compassion. He taught out of compassion. He healed out of compassion. His ministry on Earth began and ended in compassion. Jesus Christ was compassion personified.

The New Testament writers provide a comprehensive picture of how Jesus' compassion directed His ministry. A story in Mark 6 shows how the compassion of Jesus led Him to teach the multitudes.

> *So, as He stepped ashore, He saw a huge crowd and had compassion on them, because they were like sheep without a shepherd. Then He began to teach them many things.*
> Mark 6:34

Here, the compassion of Jesus is focused on the spiritual needs of the people. The phrase "sheep without a shepherd" is an Old Testament picture of Israel without spiritual leadership. Jesus, of course, proclaimed that He was the Good Shepherd who would lead His people out of their spiritual wilderness.

On three occasions Jesus used the word *compassion* in His teaching. In all three cases, the word is found in a parable. One is the parable of the lost son found in Luke 15. *Compassion* is used to describe the loving father when he sees his erring son return home.

> *But while the son was still a long way off, his father saw him and was filled with compassion. He ran, threw his arms around his neck, and kissed him.* Luke 15:20

The father's compassion compels him to run and embrace the son whom he loves. The picture is that of a loving Heavenly Father who rejoices when his children return in obedience to His will for their lives.

A second parable in which Jesus uses the word *compassion* is the story of the compassionate king in Matthew 18. Peter asked Jesus a question about the limits of forgiveness. Jesus responds with a direct answer but then shares the parable to reinforce His point. The king has compassion for a servant who could not pay the debt his debt and forgives the loan.

> *At this, the slave fell facedown before him and said, 'Be patient with me, and I will pay you everything!' Then the master of that slave had compassion, released him, and for gave him the loan.* Matthew 18:26, 27

Jesus was always concerned that His hearers understand the truth that God is no respecter of persons. The neighbor is anyone who is in need. Soon they would not only hear His teaching, but they would also see His compassion as He died for their sins on the cross.

On at least two other occasions, Jesus used the word *compassion* in His teaching. In both incidents, Jesus quoted the Old Testament prophet Hosea. In the first case, Jesus had just called Matthew the tax collector to join Him in ministry. Soon after, Jesus was sitting at a meal with several tax collectors and other "sinners" and the disciples. When the Pharisees saw Jesus eating with these undesirables, they asked the disciples why. Jesus overheard the question and responded.

> *But when Jesus heard this, He said, "It is not those who are healthy who need a physician, but those who are sick. But go and learn what this means: 'I DESIRE COMPASSION, AND NOT SACRIFICE,' for I did not come to call the righteous, but sinners."* Matthew 9:12, 13

The second time Jesus quoted Hosea's word on compassion was on the Sabbath when He and His disciples were eating from the grain fields. Again, the Pharisees noted that they were breaking the ceremonial law. Jesus reminds them that David ate the consecrated bread in the house of God which had been designated for the priest alone. Then He gave them this word.

> *Or have you not read in the Law, that on the Sabbath the priests in the temple break the Sabbath and are innocent? But I say to you that something greater than the temple is here. But if you had known what this means, 'I DESIRE COMPASSION, AND NOT A SACRIFICE,' you would not have condemned the innocent.* Matthew 12:5-7

Jesus, of course, is trying to teach them a more excellent way, the way of compassion.

In Mark 10:17 Jesus taught the multitudes and small groups out of His compassion for them to know God. At times, however, His desire to teach the truths of God led Him to encounters with individuals. These stories are powerful reminders that salvation comes one person at a time. One of the most well-known of these encounters was the meeting that Jesus had with the rich young ruler.

> As He was setting out on a journey, a man ran up to Him and knelt before Him, and asked Him, "Good Teacher, what shall I do to inherit eternal life?" And Jesus said to him, "Why do you call Me good? No one is good except God alone. You know the commandments, 'DO NOT MURDER, DO NOT COMMIT ADULTERY, DO NOT STEAL, DO NOT BEAR FALSE WITNESS, Do not defraud, HONOR YOUR FATHER AND MOTHER.'" And he said to Him, "Teacher, I have kept all these things from my youth up." Looking at him, Jesus felt a love for him and said to him, "One thing you lack: go and sell all you possess and give to the poor, and you will have treasure in heaven; and come, follow Me." Mark 10:17-21

Jesus felt a great love for this young man who was searching for truth. Evidently, his search was genuine as he kneels before Jesus and acknowledges Him as a good teacher. With great compassion Jesus tells the young man what he needs to do: sell all and follow the Master.

In the case of the rich young ruler, the encounter was initiated by the searcher. On another occasion, the opportunity came to Him by way of the religious leaders as they brought to Jesus the woman caught in adultery. The Scribes and Pharisees, according to Scripture, were trying to find some way to accuse Jesus of a crime.

The Law was clear in this case. The woman should be stoned to death for her sin. Initially, Jesus seems to agree with the woman's accusers. He suggests, however, that the one who was without sin should cast the first stone. Then Jesus begins writing in the dirt, an intriguing action that has fascinated scholars for millennia. One by one the accusers leave the temple complex. Jesus remains and engages the woman in a brief but life-changing conversation.

> *When Jesus stood up, He said to her, "Woman, where are they? Has no one condemned you?" "No one, Lord," she answered. "Neither do I condemn you," said Jesus. "Go, and from now on do not sin anymore."* John 8:10, 11

The woman must have been amazed at the great love and compassion that Jesus showed to her. Jesus used the opportunity to teach the way of repentance, forgiveness, and restoration.

The rich young ruler came to Jesus. The woman caught in adultery was brought to Jesus. But on a third occasion, Jesus' compassion drove Him to travel through a foreign land to meet one who needed to know the truth of God's great love.

The land was Samaria. Good, pious Jews would never travel through Samaria. The Samaritans were viewed as heathens who had intermarried with the Jews and corrupted Scripture. But once again, Jesus defied the religious prejudice of His day and traveled with purpose to meet a woman at a well. Though scholars disagree, John 4:4 indicates that Jesus needed to go through Samaria.

And He must need to go through Samaria. John 4:4 KJV

The truth was that Jesus did not have to go through Samaria. There was the highly traveled route to the east that most religious Jews took to avoid contact with the Samaritans. It seems most likely that His compassion drove Him to travel there to meet this woman He did not know and share with her the good news of God's love.

Jesus teaches the woman about the "living water" and the "gift of God", and then reveals to her that He is the Messiah. It is obvious from the text that the woman is captivated by Jesus as He tells her all about her life. She then runs to her village and tells everyone to come and see this man who could be the Messiah.

> *His acts of compassion had a great impact on the people. Everywhere He went people were touched by His great love.*

The great compassion of Jesus to teach and transform lives drove Him that day to seek out the lost in Samaria.

The teachings of Jesus on compassion were significant and most likely moved many people to service. But His acts of compassion also had a great impact on the people. Jesus was the embodiment of compassion. Everywhere He went people were touched by His great love. His compassion was poured out upon the single soul and the multitudes. He blessed the Jew and the Roman with His compassion. Those who write dictionaries could easily define compassion simply as, "Jesus Christ."

On more than one occasion the gospel writers record stories of Jesus' compassion for the multitudes. One such case is found in Matthew 15. The story of the feeding of the 4,000 includes Jesus' compassion for the spiritual needs, the special needs, and the simple needs of the people.

Jesus had been teaching for three days, sharing the good news of the kingdom. He had healed many who were ill, blind, and crippled. But there was a problem. The people were hungry, and Jesus did not want them to leave without eating.

> *Then Jesus called his disciples to him and said, "I have compassion on the crowd because they have been with me now three days and have nothing to eat. And I am unwilling to send them away hungry, lest they faint on the way."*
> Matthew 15:32

When the disciples heard of Jesus' concern, they spoke without thinking or believing that a solution was within their means. Jesus, of course, had a plan. He had them gather up the meager amount of food that could be found in the crowd, blessed it, and then performed the miracle, feeding the entire multitude.

The feeding of the multitude was the result of Jesus' great compassion. He was always sensitive to the needs of people and more than that, He cared deeply about meeting their needs. His compassion for the multitudes is evidence that He cares for all people. The crowd that day most likely included Jews and Greeks, bond and free, and every other classification imaginable. But Jesus had compassion on them all.

Perhaps the most poignant stories of Jesus' compassion are of the individual encounters He had with people in need. They are some of the most powerful, captivating, and inspiring stories in all of Scripture. Human tragedies are transformed into abundant living. Hopelessness is turned into rejoicing. Death is conquered by new life, all a result of love and compassion from the heart of Jesus.

The result of Jesus' compassion was often physical healing. Jesus was moved by the suffering of people. He understood how physical distress affected the psychological, the emotional, and even the spiritual aspects of a person's being. Jesus loved people so much that He healed.

Very early and throughout His ministry, Jesus showed His compassion by healing those with leprosy. Lepers were among the most rejected and despised in society. They were abandoned by their families, banned from participation in the community of faith, and doomed to suffer miserable lives and deaths.

For some, it was His compassion for the leper that amazed them the most. Jesus spoke with lepers. Touched lepers and, yes, healed lepers. Mark records one of those encounters.

> *And a leper came to Jesus, beseeching Him and falling on his knees before Him, and saying, "If You are willing, You can make me clean." Moved with compassion, Jesus stretched out His hand and touched him, and said to him,*

"I am willing; be cleansed." Immediately the leprosy left
Him and he was cleansed.   Mark 1:40-42 NASB

The drama of the scene is incredible. The man's appeal is so desperate and yet so humble. He believes that Jesus is able to heal him, but he appeals to the Lord's heart. Jesus, again, is moved with compassion. He answers the man's appeal by saying in essence, "Yes. I am willing to heal you sir" and immediately the leper is made whole. How amazing it must have been to witness the compassion of Jesus heal a leper.

The gospel narratives record repeatedly, examples of the compassionate Jesus alleviating the suffering of the blind, the lame, the possessed, and more.

As He stepped ashore, He saw a huge crowd, felt
compassion for them, and healed their sick.
Matthew 14:14

Moved with compassion, Jesus touched their eyes.
Immediately they could see, and they followed Him.
Matthew 20:34

Jesus was also moved by compassion to bring relief to the bereaved. As Jesus entered the city of Nain, he saw a funeral procession. The only son of a widow had died. In that day, the loss of the son meant a life of poverty and despair for his mother. She would have no means of support. When Jesus understood the gravity of the situation, He was moved with compassion and His compassion moved Him in a most incredible way.

When the Lord saw her, He felt compassion for her, and
said to her, "Do not weep." And He came up and
touched the coffin; and the bearers came to a halt. And He
said, "Young man, I say to you, arise!" [15] *The dead man sat*
up and began to speak. And Jesus gave him back to his
mother. Luke 7:13-15 NASB

One of the most striking examples of Jesus' compassion is found in the story of His friend Lazarus. Jesus had a special relationship with Lazarus and his family. He loved them dearly. When Jesus arrived at the home, He was overcome emotionally and began to weep. Those around the family noted how much Jesus loved Lazarus. As they made their way to the tomb, Jesus commanded that the stone be removed, and He began to pray.

…Then Jesus raised His eyes, and said, "Father, I thank
You that You have heard Me. I knew that You always
hear Me; but because of the people standing around I said
it, so that they may believe that You sent Me." When He
had said these things, He cried out with a loud voice, "Laza-
rus, come forth." The man who had died came forth,
bound hand and foot with wrappings, and his face was
wrapped around with a cloth. Jesus said to them, "Unbind
him, and let him go." John 11:41b-44 NASB

This powerful scene shows us the depths of Jesus' compassion. He weeps with those who weep. He feels their sorrow and His compassion moves Him to bring even the dead back to life.

The compassion of Jesus was poured out on so many during His time on Earth. His compassion drove Him to teach, to heal, to comfort, and more. But the ultimate expression of His boundless compassion is found in the cross of Calvary. The passion of Christ was a direct result of the compassion of Christ.

His great compassion is seen in His concern for the immediate and the eternal. First, Jesus is concerned about those around Him, particularly His mother, Mary. Most scholars agree that Joseph had died by the time of the crucifixion. Jesus has compassion for His mother and asks the disciples to care for her. Writhing in pain, He is still thinking of others above Himself.

Jesus also has compassion on one of the criminals being crucified. The thief asks Jesus to remember him when He came into His kingdom. Jesus had compassion on the man and promised him eternal life. Again, Jesus is focused on the needs of others rather than His own need.

A third expression of the compassion of Jesus is seen in the prayer He offers for the soldiers who were gambling for His garments. Others would have expressed disgust, but Jesus asks the Father to forgive the men for their heartless actions.

The greatest expression of the compassion of Jesus on the cross, however, is the fact that He died for the sins of mankind. Bible scholars have written thousands of volumes on every aspect, every nuance of the meaning of His death. They

> *The greatest expression of Jesus' compassion was the fact that He died for the sins of mankind.*

have developed systematic ways of understanding the atonement and its implications both for this world and the world to come.

As important as the meaning of His death is, however, perhaps the motive is just as important. Why did Jesus die on the cross? Some would argue that He died in obedience to the Father's will. He did have a deep desire to be about His Father's business. That is most certainly true. But the greatest motive for Jesus was His compassion. He died because He loved. His compassion for people was so great that He willingly laid down His life for theirs. He cared for people so much that He paid the debt for their sins. That is truly the heart of Jesus.

... visit orphans and widows in their affliction
James 1:27

5   *Compassion In The New Testament*

Compassion is a central theme that runs throughout the New Testament, reflecting the heart of God and the character of Christ. From the Gospels to the Epistles, we see compassion exemplified, taught, and commanded as an essential virtue for followers of Jesus. This chapter will explore how compassion is portrayed and emphasized across the various sections of the New Testament.

Compassion In the Teachings Of Jesus

Throughout the Gospels, Jesus imparts numerous teachings that highlight the transformative power of compassion, challenging His followers to embody this godly virtue in their lives. This chapter will provide a discussion of selected teachings which highlight various aspects of Jesus' teachings on compassion.

In the Sermon on the Mount, spanning Matthew 5-7, Jesus delivers a powerful and transformative message that reshapes conventional ethical norms and calls His followers to embody a new and radical vision of compassionate

> *In the Sermon on the Mount Jesus calls His followers to embody a new, radical vision of compassionate living.*

living. At the heart of this sermon lies a profound emphasis on mercy and compassion as foundational virtues in the kingdom of God. Jesus blesses the merciful, declaring, "Blessed are the merciful, for they will be shown mercy" (Matthew 5:7). This beatitude underscores the reciprocal nature of compassion—those who extend mercy to others will themselves receive mercy, reflecting God's gracious and compassionate character.

The Sermon on the Mount also emphasizes the importance of integrity and sincerity in showing compassion. Jesus warns against performing righteous acts just to be noticed by others (Matthew 6:1-4), urging His disciples instead to develop a genuine compassion that comes from a pure heart. This inner transformation is crucial for truly reflecting God's character of mercy and love, ensuring that compassionate actions are driven by genuine care for others rather than the desire for external approval or recognition.

Moreover, the Sermon on the Mount presents a vision of compassionate living that extends beyond individual relationships to encompass care for all those in need. Jesus' teachings on caring for the poor and needy (Matthew 25:31-46) emphasize the ethical imperative of compassionate action towards those in need. By feeding the hungry, clothing the naked, and visiting the imprisoned, disciples demonstrate their commitment to justice and mercy, reflecting God's compassionate concern for the least of these.

The Sermon on the Mount stands as a foundational text in Christian ethics, articulating a radical vision of compassionate living that challenges disciples to embody God's gracious and compassionate character in their interactions with others. By practicing compassion authentically and sacrificially, disciples bear witness to God's kingdom of love and justice, manifesting His transformative power in their communities and beyond.

Jesus also taught about compassion through word stories or parables. One of the most renowned parables on compassion is the Parable of the Good Samaritan (Luke 10:25-37). In this narrative, Jesus responds to a question about who qualifies as a neighbor by recounting a story of a Samaritan who shows compassion towards a wounded man left by the roadside. The Samaritan not only tends to the man's wounds but also provides for his care.

The Parable of the Good Samaritan offers profound lessons on compassion that remain relevant and impactful today. The parable teaches us that compassion knows no boundaries. The Samaritan, despite cultural and religious differences, demonstrated compassion towards a stranger in need. This teaches us that compassion should extend beyond familiar circles and comfort zones to encompass all humanity.

We are also taught that biblical compassion is not passive sympathy but active intervention. The Samaritan took practical steps to help the wounded man, highlighting the importance of tangible acts of kindness and support. Remember, actions speak louder than words.

The parable also teaches the truth that compassion most often requires sacrifice. The Samaritan sacrificed his time, resources, and comfort to care for the injured man. True compassion often involves personal cost and a willingness to inconvenience ourselves for the sake of others.

We learn another important lesson here. Compassion breaks down barriers and everyone is our neighbor. In Jesus' time, Samaritans were often despised by Jews, yet the Samaritan in the parable goes beyond prejudice and societal norms to demonstrate compassion. This challenges us to overcome prejudices and stereotypes in our interactions with others.

> *Compassion breaks down barriers. Jesus teaches us that everyone is our neighbor.*

Jesus expands the definition of neighbor beyond geographical or social boundaries to include anyone in need. He teaches us to view every person as a potential recipient of our compassion, regardless of their background or circumstances.

Perhaps most importantly we learn here that compassion involves empathy. The Samaritan "had compassion" (Luke 10:33) upon seeing the injured man. This suggests that true compassion starts with the heart, putting oneself in another's shoes, and understanding their pain or struggles. Caring is the essence of compassion.

Courage is another lesson learned from the parable of the Good Samaritan. The Samaritan risked potential danger and inconvenience to help the injured man. This teaches us that compassion sometimes requires having the courage to stand up for what is right, to intervene in difficult situations, and to challenge injustice or indifference.

At least one additional lesson can be gleaned from this parable. Compassion reflects the character of God. Ultimately, the story reveals God's compassionate nature and challenges us to reflect His character in our interactions with others. It encourages us to cultivate a compassionate heart that mirrors God's love, mercy, and care for all people. Hear God's call today to be like the Samaritan.

The Parable of the Sheep and the Goats, found in Matthew 25:31-46, provides a powerful framework for understanding the importance of compassion ministries. In this parable, Jesus portrays a scene of final judgment where individuals are separated into two groups, the sheep, who are blessed and welcomed into the kingdom, and the goats, who are condemned.

The parable begins with the Son of Man coming in glory, accompanied by angels, to judge all nations. He separates people as a shepherd separates sheep from goats, placing the sheep on His right and the goats on His left (Matthew 25:32-33). The criterion for this judgment is based on how they treated the "least of these brothers and sisters of mine" (Matthew 25:40, 45), emphasizing compassionate action towards those in need as a central aspect of discipleship.

Jesus identifies Himself with the hungry, thirsty, stranger, naked, sick, and imprisoned, the "least of these." He declares that those who fed the hungry, gave drink to the thirsty, welcomed strangers, clothed the naked, cared for the sick, and visited prisoners did so unto Him (Matthew 25:35-36). This identification underscores the profound spiritual significance of compassion ministries in serving Christ by serving those in need.

The parable highlights the urgency and importance of compassionate action in our Christian witness. Jesus commends the righteous (the sheep) for their acts of mercy and compassion, noting that whatever they did for the least of these, they did for Him (Matthew 25:40). This teaches us that compassion ministries are not merely optional acts of kindness but essential expressions of discipleship and obedience to Christ's teachings.

Moreover, Jesus challenges believers to evaluate their priorities and lifestyles considering God's kingdom values. It confronts the danger of neglecting the needs of the poor and vulnerable in society, reminding us that our response to those in need reflects our commitment to following Christ. Compassion ministries, therefore, compel us to actively seek justice, mercy, and restoration for those who are suffering.

Additionally, this parable underscores the holistic nature of compassion ministries in addressing both the physical and spiritual needs of individuals. Jesus not only identifies with the physical suffering of the hungry, thirsty, and sick but also with their spiritual condition. Compassion ministries, therefore, seek to meet the tangible needs of individuals while also offering spiritual support, guidance, and the hope found in the gospel of Christ.

Moreover, the parable challenges believers to engage in proactive and intentional acts of compassion, rather than passively waiting for opportunities to serve. Jesus commends the righteous for their initiative in feeding the hungry, giving drink to the thirsty, and welcoming strangers (Matthew 25:35-36), highlighting the importance of proactive compassion ministries that actively seek out and respond to the needs of others.

Additionally, Jesus challenges the church and individual believers to prioritize compassion ministries as integral to their mission and witness in the world. Jesus identifies acts of mercy and compassion as direct expressions of love for Him (Matthew 25:40), reinforcing the biblical mandate to love our neighbors as ourselves and to demonstrate God's love through practical deeds of kindness and service.

The Parable of the Sheep and the Goats provides a compelling framework for understanding the profound significance of compassion ministries in Christian discipleship. It underscores the

> *Compassion ministries embody God's kingdom values of love, mercy, and justice.*

essential role of compassionate action in serving Christ by ministering to the physical, emotional, and spiritual needs of others. Compassion ministries embody God's kingdom values of love, mercy, and justice, offering tangible expressions of Christ's love to a hurting world while preparing hearts for the eternal kingdom of God.

In addition to the Sermon on the Mount and the parables, Jesus also taught principles of compassion during certain encounters he had with various individuals. Jesus' interactions with individuals such as the woman caught in adultery (John 8:1-11) and Zacchaeus the tax collector (Luke 19:1-10) further exemplify His compassionate approach toward sinners and outcasts. In these encounters, Jesus extends forgiveness, acceptance, and a path to redemption, embodying God's compassionate stance towards those who repent and seek His grace.

Jesus' teachings on compassion in the Gospels challenge us to embody a radical ethic of love and forgiveness in our daily lives. As disciples of Jesus, we are called to follow His teachings, extending mercy and grace to all, and thereby reflecting the character of God's kingdom here on earth.

Compassion In the Acts Of The Apostles

The Acts of the Apostles vividly portrays the early church's commitment to compassion, demonstrating how the followers of Jesus carried forward His teachings and actions. One of the first acts of compassion recorded is the communal sharing of resources among believers. Acts 2:44-45 describes how "all the believers were together and had everything in common. They sold property and possessions to give to anyone who had need." This radical sharing of resources ensured that no one in the community lacked necessities, reflecting a very deep sense of mutual care and compassion.

The early Christian community's practice of sharing resources was not merely a social arrangement but a profound expression of compassion. Acts 4:32-35 further illustrates this, noting that "no one claimed that any of their possessions was their own, but they shared everything they had." This communal lifestyle was underpinned by the apostles' testimony about the resurrection of Jesus, which inspired believers to live selflessly and support one another. The distribution of resources was managed by the apostles, who ensured that those in need were cared for, embodying the compassion that Jesus had taught.

Peter, one of the leading apostles, exemplified compassionate leadership through his actions and miracles. In Acts 3:1-10, Peter and John encounter a man who had been lame from birth, begging at the temple gate. Peter, moved by compassion, tells the man, "Silver or gold I do not have, but what I do have I give you. In the name of Jesus Christ of Nazareth, walk." Peter's healing of the man not only restores his physical ability but also reintegrates him into the community, demonstrating the transformative power of compassionate action.

Peter's compassion is also evident in his preaching. After healing the lame man, Peter addresses the crowd, urging them to repent and turn to God so that their sins may be wiped out (Acts 3:19). His message is one of hope and restoration, offering spiritual healing and reconciliation with God. Peter's willingness to preach to diverse audiences, including Gentiles, as seen in his encounter with Cornelius in Acts 10, underscores his commitment to extending God's compassion to all people, regardless of their background.

The early disciples, following the example of Jesus and the apostles, engaged in various acts of compassion. Acts 6:1-7 describes how the early church addressed the needs of widows, ensuring that they received daily food distribution. This compassionate response led to the appointment of seven deacons, including Stephen, to oversee the fair distribution of resources. This action not only met the immediate needs of the widows but also promoted justice within the community.

The early disciples' evangelistic efforts were also marked by compassion. Acts 8:26-40 recounts the story of Philip and the Ethiopian eunuch. Philip, guided by the Holy Spirit, approaches the eunuch who is reading Isaiah but does not understand it. With compassion and patience, Philip explains the Scriptures and shares the good news of Jesus, leading to the eunuch's baptism. This encounter highlights the disciples' commitment to compassionate evangelism, meeting people where they are, and guiding them toward faith.

The Acts of the Apostles provide a rich tapestry of compassionate actions and teachings that shaped the early Christian community. From the communal sharing of resources to compassionate leadership, and the dedicated acts of the early disciples, compassion was a defining characteristic of the early church.

Acts also illustrates how compassion serves as a powerful and effective tool for evangelization. The early Christians' care for the sick and economically challenged drew others to faith in Christ.

Acts 5:12-16 recounts how people brought their sick to be healed by Peter, underscoring the belief that compassion and healing were intertwined in the ministry of the apostles. This compassionate outreach not

> *Acts illustrates how compassion serves as a powerful and effective tool for evangelism.*

only alleviated suffering but also demonstrated the transformative power of Christ's love, compelling others to inquire about the source of such compassion and ultimately leading many to embrace Christianity.

The Acts of the Apostles thus challenges modern Christians to uphold compassion as a cornerstone of their faith, ensuring that it remains a guiding principle in their interactions with others and in their collective witness to the world.

Acts offers timeless lessons for modern Christianity on the importance of compassion. Today, amid societal challenges and global crises, the call to compassion remains as urgent as ever. Like the early Christians, modern believers are called to embody compassion in their daily lives, reaching out to those in need and promoting unity within the community. Acts serves as a blueprint for building compassionate communities that reflect Christ's love and transform lives through acts of kindness and generosity.

Compassion In the Pauline Epistles

Compassion is a recurring theme in the Pauline Epistles, reflecting the deep love and empathy that Paul believed should characterize the Christian life. Paul's teachings on compassion provide a framework for understanding how believers are to live out their faith in a world filled with suffering and need. Here, we explore Paul's teachings on compassion, the role of the church in compassion ministry, and key passages in 1 Corinthians 13 and Romans 12 that highlight the importance of love and compassion in the Christian community.

Paul's writings consistently emphasize the importance of compassion as a reflection of God's character and as an essential aspect of Christian living. For Paul, compassion is not merely an emotional response, but a deliberate action rooted in love and motivated by a desire to alleviate the suffering of others.

In his letter to the Colossians, Paul exhorts believers to "put on compassion, kindness, humility, gentleness, and patience" (Colossians 3:12). Here, compassion is presented as part of the Christian clothing that believers must wear, signifying that it is integral to the identity of a follower of Christ. Compassion is also closely linked with other virtues such as kindness and humility, suggesting that it is a fundamental expression of love in action.

Paul's own life serves as a model of compassionate ministry. He frequently expresses his deep concern for the well-being of others, whether through his letters or during his missionary journeys. His willingness to endure hardship for the sake of others, as seen in passages like 2 Corinthians 11:23-28, illustrates his commitment to compassionate service. Paul understood that compassion required sacrifice and that it was an essential expression of the gospel.

Paul saw the church as the primary vehicle for the expression of God's compassion in the world. The church is called to be a community of love, where members care for one another and extend that care to the broader society. Compassionate ministry is not just an individual responsibility but a collective mission of the church.

Two key passages in Paul's letters, 1 Corinthians 13 and Romans 12, provide profound insights into the nature of compassion and its centrality to the Christian life.

First Corinthians 13, often referred to as the "Love Chapter," is one of the most well-known passages in the New Testament. Paul eloquently describes the characteristics of love,

> *Paul asserts that all spiritual gifts and acts of service are meaningless without love.*

placing it at the center of the Christian life. He begins by asserting that all spiritual gifts and acts of service are meaningless without love: "If I speak in the tongues of men and of angels, but have not love, I am a noisy gong or a clanging cymbal" (1 Corinthians 13:1).

Paul's description of love in verses 4-7 is a blueprint for compassion: "Love is patient and kind; love does not envy or boast; it is not arrogant or rude. It does not insist on its way; it is not irritable or resentful; it does not rejoice at wrongdoing but rejoices with the truth. Love bears all things, believes all things, hopes all things, endures all things." Each of these qualities reflects a compassionate heart, one that is concerned with the well-being of others and willing to endure hardship for their sake.

The chapter concludes with Paul's assertion that love is the greatest of all virtues: "So now faith, hope, and love abide, these three; but the greatest of these is love" (1 Corinthians 13:13). This statement underscores the importance of love, and by extension, compassion, in the life of a Christian. Without love, all other virtues and actions lose their meaning and value.

In Romans 12, Paul provides practical instructions for living out the Christian faith, with a strong emphasis on love and compassion. Paul exhorts believers to "rejoice with those who rejoice, weep with those who weep" (Romans 12:15). This verse encapsulates the essence of compassion—entering the joys and sorrows of others, sharing in their experiences, and providing comfort and support. Compassion, according to Paul, involves a deep identification with the experiences of others, reflecting the love of Christ who "bore our griefs and carried our sorrows" (Isaiah 53:4).

Compassion is a central theme in the Pauline Epistles, rooted in the character of God and the love of Christ. Paul's teachings on compassion challenge believers to live out their faith through acts of love and mercy, both within the church and in broader society. The church, as the body of Christ, is called to be a community where compassion is practiced and extended to those in need. In following Paul's teachings, Christians are called to be agents of God's compassion in the world, reflecting His love through their actions and attitudes.

Compassion In the Epistles Of James And John

Compassion ministry is a crucial aspect of Christian discipleship, vividly portrayed in the New Testament through the Epistles of James and John. These epistles offer practical guidance and theological insights on how believers are to express their faith through acts of love and compassion. This section focuses on the teachings of compassion ministry with an emphasis on the relationship between faith and works in James and the themes of love and compassion in the Johannine letters.

Both James and John emphasize the importance of compassion ministry as an essential expression of Christian faith. However, each approaches the topic with a unique perspective, contributing to a holistic understanding of how believers should engage in compassionate service. The Epistle of James is renowned for its emphasis on the practical outworking of faith, particularly through acts of compassion and mercy.

James consistently highlights the necessity of caring for the most vulnerable members of society, such as orphans and widows, as a true expression of pure religion. In James 1:27, he writes, "Religion that is pure and undefiled before God the Father is this: to visit orphans and widows in their affliction, and to keep oneself unstained from the world." This verse underscores that true faith is not only about personal holiness but also about actively engaging in compassion ministry.

James further challenges believers by pointing out the futility of faith that does not result in compassionate action. In James 2:14-17, he addresses the scenario of a believer who encounters a brother or sister in need but offers only words of goodwill without providing practical help. James declares that such faith is dead, stating, "If a brother or sister is poorly clothed and lacking in daily food, and one of you says to them, 'Go in peace, be warmed and filled,' without giving them the things needed for the body, what good is that?" (James 2:15-16). For James, compassion ministry is not optional but an essential demonstration of living faith.

The Epistle of James presents a powerful argument for the necessity of works, particularly compassionate works, as an expression of genuine faith. James's teachings directly challenge any notion of faith that does not result in action. James asserts that faith without works is dead, using the example of someone who professes faith but fails to provide for a brother or sister in need. He writes, "So also faith by itself, if it does not have works, is dead" (James 2:17). James insists that genuine faith will naturally produce works, particularly in the context of compassion ministry. The legitimacy of one's faith, according to James, is proven by the works it produces, especially in caring for those in need.

James's emphasis on the relationship between faith and works is not a call to legalism but a call to authentic Christian living. He uses the examples of Abraham and Rahab to illustrate that their faith was made complete by their actions (James 2:21-26). For James, compassion ministry is not just a good deed but a vital expression of living faith, revealing the authenticity of a believer's relationship with God.

The Johannine letters, particularly 1 John, are deeply concerned with the theme of love, which is at the heart of compassion ministry. John's writings emphasize that love is the defining characteristic of a true Christian, and this love must be expressed through acts of compassion.

In 1 John 3:16-18, John provides a profound call to compassion ministry: "By this, we know love, that He laid down His life for us, and we ought to lay down our lives for the brothers. But if anyone has the world's goods

> *Genuine love must be manifested in practical acts of compassion, meeting needs in tangible ways.*

and sees his brother in need, yet closes his heart against him, how does God's love abide in him? Little children, let us not love in word or talk but in deed and truth." This passage highlights that genuine love, inspired by Christ's sacrifice, must be manifested in practical acts of compassion, meeting the needs of others in tangible ways.

John also repeatedly emphasizes that love is the evidence of knowing God, and this love must be demonstrated through compassion ministry. In 1 John 4:7-12, he writes that love is from God, and those who know God must love others as God loves them. This teaching underscores the inseparability of love for God and love for others, with compassion ministry serving as the practical expression of that love.

John's emphasis on love as the defining mark of a Christian also extends to the community of believers. In 1 John 4:7-12, he writes that love is from God, and everyone who loves is born of God and knows God. This passage emphasizes that love is not merely an emotion but a divine attribute that must be reflected in the believer's life through compassion ministry. Love and compassion are inseparable in John's theology; to love God is to love others, and to love others is to engage in acts of compassion.

John also warns against the dangers of failing to love. In 1 John 4:20, he states, "If anyone says, 'I love God,' and hates his brother, he is a liar; for he who does not love his brother whom he has seen cannot love God whom he has not seen." This strong language underscores the seriousness with which John views the connection between love for God and love for others. Compassion ministry, in the Johannine letters, is the true test of love, revealing whether God's love truly abides in a believer.

The Epistles of James and John offer a compelling and complementary vision of compassion ministry within the Christian life. James emphasizes the inseparability of faith and works, particularly in the context of caring for those in need, making it clear that true faith must manifest in compassion ministry. John, on the other hand, presents love as the essence of God and the defining characteristic of a Christian, insisting that this love must be demonstrated through practical acts of compassion.

Together, these epistles challenge believers to embody their faith through compassionate service, making compassion ministry an essential aspect of the Christian life. By following these teachings, believers not only fulfill our calling but also reflect the love of Christ to a world in need, living out the true essence of our faith.

The New Testament foundations of compassion ministries reveal a profound and enduring call for Christians to embody the love of Christ through tangible acts of service. Rooted in the teachings of Jesus, as well as the writings of the Apostles, compassion is shown to be an integral aspect of the Christian faith, one that cannot be separated from authentic discipleship. The New

Testament emphasizes that true religion involves caring for the vulnerable and integrating faith with works.

By building compassionate communities and implementing strategies that address basic human needs, the church can faithfully reflect the heart of God in a world that desperately needs His love. These foundations challenge and inspire contemporary ministries to not only preach the gospel but also to live it out in ways that transform lives and communities, bringing hope and healing in the name of Christ.

...in the encouragement of the Holy Spirit
Acts 9:31

6   *The Role of the Holy Spirit*

The Bible outlines several key roles that the Holy Spirit plays in compassion ministry. These roles are essential in empowering believers to serve others effectively and reflect the love of Christ in their actions. Here are some of the primary roles of the Holy Spirit in compassion ministry.

First, the Holy Spirit provides guidance and direction to believers, leading them to opportunities where they can serve others compassionately. In Acts 8:29, the Holy Spirit instructs Philip to approach the Ethiopian eunuch, resulting in a significant moment of ministry. This role of the Spirit is crucial in helping believers discern where their efforts and resources can make the most impact.

The Holy Spirit also empowers believers to carry out acts of compassion beyond their natural abilities. In Acts 1:8, Jesus promises that the Holy Spirit will come upon His followers and give them power to be His witnesses. This empowerment enables believers to serve others with boldness, strength, and endurance, even in challenging circumstances.

In addition, the Holy Spirit bestows spiritual gifts on believers that are vital for compassionate ministry. According to 1 Corinthians 12:4-11, the Spirit distributes various gifts such as wisdom, knowledge, healing, and mercy, which are essential for effective ministry. These gifts enable believers to meet the diverse needs of those they serve.

The Holy Spirit also cultivates a heart of compassion within believers, reflecting God's compassion for humanity. Romans 5:5 states that "God's love has been poured into our hearts through the Holy Spirit who has been given to us." This divine love compels believers to act with compassion toward others, especially those who are suffering or marginalized.

In compassion ministry, the Holy Spirit actively works as the Comforter, bringing comfort and strength to both those who serve and those who are served. John 14:26 identifies the Holy Spirit as the Comforter or Advocate, who teaches and reminds believers of Jesus' teachings. This role is essential in compassion ministry, as the Holy Spirit not only empowers believers to extend Christ-like compassion but also sustains them with encouragement and peace. This divine support enables them to persevere in their service, providing both the inner strength to carry on and the comfort needed to minister effectively to those in need.

Another key role of the Holy Spirit is empowering believers to be witnesses of God's love through their acts of compassion. In Acts

4:31, the disciples are filled with the Holy Spirit and speak the word of God boldly. Compassion ministry often opens doors for sharing the gospel, and the Holy Spirit enables believers to bear witness to Christ's love through their actions.

The Holy Spirit also inspires and empowers believers to give generously in compassion ministry. Acts 4:32-35 describes how the early believers, filled with the Holy Spirit, shared everything they had, ensuring that no one was in need. This spirit of generosity is crucial for sustaining ministry efforts and meeting the needs of the community.

The Holy Spirit also produces joy in the hearts of those engaged in compassion ministry. Romans 14:17 links the kingdom of God with joy in the Holy Spirit. This joy sustains believers as they serve others, making their ministry not just a duty but a source of deep fulfillment and delight.

Scripture also teaches that the Holy Spirit is actively involved in the healing and restoration process in compassion ministry. First Corinthians 12:9 mentions the gift of healing given by the Spirit, which is essential in ministries that address emotional and spiritual wounds. The Spirit's healing power brings wholeness to those who are broken and suffering.

The Holy Spirit reveals God's deep compassion to believers, helping them to understand and internalize His love for people. Romans 5:5 tells us that God's love has been poured into our hearts through the Holy Spirit who has been given to us. This revelation motivates believers to show the same compassion to others that they have received from God. By understanding the depth of God's love, believers are empowered to extend that love in their ministry to the hurting and the lost.

The Holy Spirit plays a multifaceted role in compassion ministry, from guiding and empowering believers to fostering unity and creating compassionate communities. Through the Spirit, believers are equipped to serve others in ways that reflect God's love and bring healing, justice, and hope to a broken world.

PART 2
Practical Applications

...clothe yourselves with compassion and kindness
Colossians 3:12

7   *Cultivating Personal Compassion*

Cultivating personal compassion is at the heart of Christian ministry, reflecting the transformative love of Jesus Christ in both word and deed. As Christians seek to embody Christ's teachings, the journey toward personal compassion involves both recognizing and overcoming barriers that may hinder the practice of empathy and kindness. Addressing these challenges is essential for developing a compassionate heart that mirrors Christ's love for all people.

This chapter explores common barriers to personal Christian compassion, such as fear, prejudice, lack of understanding, personal discomfort, and apathy, and offers practical strategies for overcoming them. By acknowledging these challenges and implementing actionable steps, we can develop a more profound and effective expression of Christian love and service through compassion ministries.

Barriers To Personal Compassion

As much as we hate to admit it, all of us face challenges to having pure hearts of compassion. Those challenges can be born out of negative views held by our families or communities regarding the poor. Whatever the source of our challenges, we must address any barrier that prevents us from loving people with the heart of Jesus.

Fear and prejudice are common hindrances to developing a compassionate heart. Fear often arises from the unknown or unfamiliar, which can create a barrier to compassionate engagement. This fear may manifest in various forms, such as anxiety about interacting with people from diverse backgrounds, concerns about personal safety, or apprehension about not knowing how to help effectively. Fear can prevent individuals from stepping out of their comfort zones to offer support or engage with those in need.

Prejudice, on the other hand, stems from preconceived notions or biases against individuals or groups based on their race, ethnicity, socioeconomic status, or other characteristics. Prejudice can lead to unfair judgments and discriminatory attitudes, which obstruct the practice of genuine compassion. This bias often results from societal stereotypes, misinformation, or personal experiences that have shaped one's worldview.

Both fear and prejudice hinder Christian compassion because they create emotional and mental barriers that prevent individuals from fully engaging with and understanding the needs of others. Fear can make people hesitant to act, while prejudice can skew their perceptions and limit their willingness to reach out. Overcoming these two obstacles is vital to cultivating personal compassion.

A lack of understanding is another barrier to developing personal Christian compassion. A lack of understanding is a significant hindrance to developing Christian compassion, primarily because it limits one's ability to connect meaningfully with others. Compassion requires more than just a general desire to help; it demands an in-depth comprehension of the specific needs, challenges, and experiences of those one seeks to support.

When individuals lack an understanding of the complexities surrounding various social issues or cultural contexts, their efforts to assist can be misguided or insufficiently tailored to the actual needs of those they aim to help.

Moreover, a lack of understanding can perpetuate stereotypes and reinforce biases. When people are unfamiliar with different cultures or social issues, they may rely on generalized assumptions or misconceptions, which can lead to prejudiced attitudes and ineffective forms of support.

Additionally, a lack of understanding can lead to an ineffective approach to ministry and outreach. Without a thorough grasp of the specific needs and cultural contexts of the people they are trying to help, individuals and organizations may implement well-intentioned but ultimately ineffective programs. This can result in wasted resources and missed opportunities to make a meaningful impact.

A lack of understanding is a significant barrier to developing Christian compassion because it limits the effectiveness, empathy, and inclusivity of compassionate efforts. We must do all we can to know our communities and the people to whom we will provide the love and care of Jesus.

Indifference or apathy is a very significant barrier to developing true Christian compassion because it reflects a disengagement from the needs and suffering of others. When individuals are indifferent, they remain

> *Indifference or apathy is a very significant barrier to developing true Christian compassion.*

detached from the experiences and struggles of those around them, often failing to recognize or respond to their needs.

This lack of emotional engagement prevents individuals from fully embodying the compassion that Jesus taught, which involves actively caring for and supporting others. Without genuine concern, efforts to help may lack sincerity or effectiveness, undermining the potential for meaningful impact.

Apathy often stems from various factors, including complacency, overload, or personal disconnection. In a world saturated with information about social issues and crises, it can be overwhelming to discern where to focus one's efforts. This can lead to a sense of helplessness or resignation, causing individuals to retreat into a state of indifference. Additionally, personal concerns and daily life distractions can create a barrier to empathy, making it difficult to prioritize the needs of others. Addressing these factors is crucial for fostering a compassionate response.

Note has been made of the fact that Scripture emphasizes the importance of active love and involvement in the lives of others. Jesus' parables, such as the Good Samaritan, underscore the call to not only recognize but also respond to the suffering of those in need. The story of the Good Samaritan illustrates that true compassion involves stepping out of one's comfort zone and actively engaging with those who are suffering, regardless of societal boundaries or personal inconvenience. Apathy contradicts this call by prioritizing personal comfort over the well-being of others, hindering the development of genuine Christian compassion.

Apathy is such a significant barrier to developing Christian compassion because it is a problem of the heart. If indifference is the barrier, something is missing in one's relationship with the Lord. Jesus cared about us. We must care about others.

Feeling out of one's comfort zone can be another significant barrier to developing personal compassion. This discomfort often manifests as reluctance or hesitation to step into unfamiliar or challenging situations, which can hinder one's willingness to participate in acts of service. Understanding why this barrier exists is essential for addressing it and fostering a more compassionate and impactful ministry.

One primary reason feeling out of one's comfort zone is a barrier is that it triggers psychological discomfort. This discomfort can stem from fears of inadequacy, failure, or social awkwardness.

When individuals are confronted with situations that are outside their usual experiences or expertise, they may feel anxious about their ability to perform effectively or make a positive impact.

This fear can lead to avoidance behaviors, where individuals choose not to engage in ministry opportunities that provoke these uncomfortable feelings. Such avoidance limits their ability to serve others and grow in their compassionate capacities.

Emotional resistance may also play a role in why stepping out of one's comfort zone can be a barrier. Compassion ministry often involves confronting distressing realities and engaging with people who are experiencing significant hardships. This emotional intensity can be overwhelming and provoke resistance, particularly when individuals are not accustomed to dealing with such profound issues. The fear of being emotionally drained or exposed to difficult emotions can lead to reluctance to participate fully in ministry activities, thereby impeding the development of genuine compassion.

Another factor contributing to this barrier is the perception of risks associated with stepping outside one's comfort zone. Engaging in unfamiliar environments or working with diverse groups can sometimes involve risks related to safety, social dynamics, or personal well-being. These perceived risks can exacerbate feelings of discomfort and create a mental block that prevents individuals from acting. The apprehension about potential negative outcomes can overshadow the potential benefits of compassionate engagement, making it challenging to overcome the initial barrier of discomfort.

Stepping out of one's comfort zone often requires a level of confidence that many individuals may not initially feel. The uncertainty of handling new situations or interacting with unfamiliar communities can undermine self-confidence, making it difficult to take the first step toward involvement. This lack of confidence can deter individuals from participating in compassion ministry, as they may doubt their ability to contribute effectively or be concerned about their perceived inadequacies.

Comfort zones provide a sense of stability and predictability, which many individuals find reassuring. Stepping outside of these boundaries necessitates a willingness to embrace change and uncertainty.

> *Stepping outside comfort zones requires a willingness to embrace change and uncertainty.*

Resistance to change can manifest as reluctance to try new approaches, adapt to different cultural contexts, or engage in unfamiliar service activities. This resistance can prevent individuals from expanding their horizons and embracing the transformative potential of compassion ministry.

Finally, the barrier of feeling out of one's comfort zone can directly impact the effectiveness of compassion ministry. When individuals are not fully engaged or willing to confront discomfort, their efforts may lack depth and authenticity. Compassion requires not just action but also an open-hearted approach that embraces the complexities of others' lives. If individuals are unwilling to push past their comfort zones, their ministry efforts may be superficial or limited, reducing the overall impact on those they aim to serve.

Practical Steps For Cultivating Personal Compassion

Volunteering regularly is a practical and impactful step toward cultivating personal compassion. When individuals engage in service activities that align with their passions and skills, they not only contribute to positive change in their communities but also nurture empathy, kindness, and a deeper understanding of others' needs.

One of the key benefits of volunteering is the opportunity to connect with causes and issues that resonate personally. Whether it's working with children, caring for animals, assisting the elderly, or supporting environmental initiatives, choosing activities that align with one's passions creates a sense of purpose and fulfillment. This alignment fosters genuine compassion as individuals invest their time and energy in making a meaningful difference in areas they care deeply about.

Moreover, volunteering provides practical experience in showing compassion through action. By actively participating in service activities, individuals develop empathy as they interact with diverse groups of people facing various challenges. This hands-on experience allows volunteers to witness firsthand the impact of their efforts, reinforcing their commitment to compassionate service and inspiring continued involvement.

Regular volunteering also cultivates humility and gratitude. Serving others humbly acknowledges the inherent dignity and worth of every individual, regardless of their circumstances. It encourages volunteers to see beyond themselves and their own needs, fostering a perspective of gratitude for their blessings and a desire to share those blessings with others who may be less fortunate.

Additionally, volunteering offers opportunities for personal growth and skill development. Engaging in service activities allows individuals to learn new skills, expand their knowledge, and develop qualities such as patience, resilience, and effective communication. These experiences not only enhance personal capabilities but also equip volunteers with valuable tools for building meaningful relationships and making a positive impact in their communities.

Volunteering regularly can also be a catalyst for building relationships and fostering a sense of community. Working alongside like-minded individuals who share a passion for service creates bonds based on shared values and goals. These relationships provide support, encouragement, and camaraderie, enhancing the volunteer experience and reinforcing the importance of compassion and collaboration in achieving common objectives.

Furthermore, volunteering promotes a broader understanding of the great challenges affecting communities. By engaging directly with those individuals and families experiencing poverty, homelessness, illness, or other hardships, volunteers gain insight into the root causes of these issues and the barriers that prevent people from thriving. This awareness helps volunteers minister more effectively making a greater impact on families and their communities.

Volunteering regularly also helps individuals develop a sense of responsibility and stewardship toward their communities. It encourages a proactive approach to making a positive impact and inspires individuals to

> *Volunteering helps develop a sense of responsibility and stewardship toward one's community.*

take the initiative in addressing community needs. By actively participating in service activities, volunteers demonstrate their commitment to being agents of change and contributing to the common good.

Volunteering regularly is a transformative journey that nurtures personal compassion, empathy, and a commitment to service. By engaging in activities that align with their passions and skills, individuals not only contribute to improving the lives of others but also cultivate humility, gratitude, and a deeper understanding of social issues. Regular volunteering builds relationships, fosters community, promotes personal growth, and empowers individuals to advocate for justice and equality. Ultimately, it is through compassionate action and service that individuals can make a meaningful difference in their communities and embody the values of love, kindness, and solidarity.

Practice active listening is a foundational principle in developing personal Christian compassion, as it emphasizes empathy, understanding, and respect for others. When individuals engage in active listening, they intentionally focus on comprehending the perspectives, emotions, and experiences of those they interact with, without rushing to judgment or interrupting. This approach fosters genuine connections and demonstrates Christ-like love in practical ways.

Active listening begins with being fully present in conversations. It involves giving undivided attention to the speaker, maintaining eye contact, and showing non-verbal cues such as nodding or leaning forward to indicate attentiveness. By creating a supportive environment where individuals feel heard and valued, active listening lays the groundwork for meaningful dialogue and mutual understanding.

Furthermore, active listening requires setting aside preconceived notions or biases and approaching interactions with an open mind. This willingness to suspend judgment allows individuals to empathize with others' perspectives, even if they differ from their own. It reflects Jesus' teaching to "love your neighbor as yourself" (Mark 12:31), embodying compassion and acceptance regardless of differences.

Practicing active listening also involves asking clarifying questions and paraphrasing to ensure accurate understanding. By seeking clarification and restating what has been said in one's own words, individuals demonstrate a genuine desire to understand and validate the speaker's thoughts and feelings. This process promotes empathy and deepens connections, fostering a sense of trust and mutual respect.

Moreover, active listening includes acknowledging emotions and validating feelings expressed by others. It involves empathetic responses that convey understanding and compassion, such as saying, "I can see why you feel that way," or "That must be difficult for you." Validating emotions creates space for individuals to share openly and honestly, promoting healing and connection in moments of vulnerability.

In Christian practice, active listening is not only about hearing words but also discerning the deeper needs and desires of the heart. It involves listening with spiritual sensitivity and discernment, guided by the Holy Spirit. This approach allows individuals to offer prayerful support, encouragement, and guidance based on God's love and wisdom, nurturing spiritual growth and healing in others.

Furthermore, active listening cultivates humility and a willingness to learn from others. It recognizes that everyone has unique experiences and perspectives shaped by their backgrounds and life journeys. By valuing diverse voices and seeking to understand different viewpoints, individuals embrace humility and broaden their understanding of God's inclusive love for all people.

Practicing active listening also strengthens relationships and builds bridges of trust within Christian communities. By creating a culture of respectful listening and mutual support, individuals foster unity and collaboration in pursuing shared goals of justice, mercy, and compassion. This collaborative spirit reflects Jesus' prayer for his followers to be one, as he and the Father are one (John 17:21), united in love and purpose.

Practicing active listening is a transformative way to cultivate personal Christian compassion by fostering empathy, understanding, and respectful engagement with others. By focusing on understanding their perspectives without judgment or interruption, individuals demonstrate Christ-like love in their interactions.

Active listening also promotes meaningful dialogue, strengthens relationships, and nurtures spiritual growth, embodying the values of compassion, empathy, and humility taught by Jesus Christ. As individuals commit to listening actively and loving their neighbors as themselves, they contribute to creating communities of grace and healing where all are valued and supported in their journeys of faith.

Cultivating gratitude is another practical step toward developing Christian compassion. By regularly acknowledging and reflecting on the blessings in one's life, individuals not only enhance their sense of contentment but also become more attuned to the needs and struggles of others. This heightened awareness can serve as a powerful motivator for compassionate action, rooted in the understanding of how much one has been given.

One effective way to cultivate gratitude is through daily practices of reflection and thankfulness. Keeping a gratitude journal where you record things you are thankful for each day helps to shift focus from what is lacking to what is present and positive. This simple yet impactful practice fosters a mindset of abundance and appreciation, making individuals more conscious of their blessings and more inclined to extend generosity and kindness to others.

Furthermore, expressing gratitude regularly can deepen one's spiritual life and enhance Christian compassion. Prayerfully thanking God for His blessings and grace not only nurtures a closer relationship with Him but also reinforces the understanding that all good things come from God. This perspective encourages believers to use their blessings to bless others, aligning with Christ's teachings on loving one's neighbor and sharing with those in need.

Cultivating gratitude also involves recognizing and appreciating the support and kindness of others. When individuals acknowledge the efforts and sacrifices of friends, family, and community members, they foster a sense of connection and mutual respect. This recognition can motivate individuals to reciprocate with acts of kindness and support, thereby creating a cycle of compassion and generosity within relationships and communities.

Moreover, a gratitude-oriented perspective helps individuals remain humble and aware of their own privileges. By reflecting on their own blessings, individuals become more conscious of the disparities and challenges faced by those less fortunate. This awareness can inspire action, such as volunteering, donating to causes, or advocating for justice, driven by a desire to address the needs of others in light of their own abundance.

Engaging in community service and charitable activities is another practical manifestation of gratitude. When individuals recognize the many blessings they have, they often feel compelled to share their resources, time, and talents with others. This alignment of personal abundance with community service exemplifies Christian compassion, as it reflects Christ's call to love and serve others selflessly.

Gratitude also fosters resilience and positivity, which can enhance one's ability to engage in compassionate action. By focusing on the positives in life, individuals are better equipped to handle challenges and setbacks with grace. This positive outlook enables them to approach service and outreach with enthusiasm and perseverance, even in the face of difficulties or adversity.

Finally, cultivating gratitude can strengthen communal bonds and foster a culture of appreciation and support. In Christian communities, expressing thanks and acknowledging each other's contributions creates an environment of encouragement and mutual care. This supportive atmosphere not only enhances individual well-being but also inspires collective efforts to serve and uplift those in need, reinforcing the shared mission of embodying Christ's love.

Cultivating gratitude in our hearts is a transformative practice that significantly enhances Christian compassion. By regularly acknowledging the blessings in one's life, individuals increase their awareness of others' needs and are motivated to take compassionate action. Through practices such as keeping a gratitude journal, expressing thanks in prayer, recognizing the support of others, and engaging in community service, individuals can align their abundance with acts of kindness and generosity.

This holistic approach to gratitude not only deepens personal spiritual growth but also fosters a culture of compassion and support within communities, reflecting the love and care taught by Jesus Christ.

Seek Diverse Relationships

Seeking diverse relationships is a vital practice for cultivating Christian compassion, as it broadens perspectives and deepens empathy. Building friendships with individuals from various backgrounds enriches one's understanding of

> *Embracing diversity in relationships helps us embody the inclusive love of Christ.*

diverse cultures, experiences, and viewpoints, aligning with the Christian call to love and serve all people. By embracing diversity in relationships, individuals can more fully embody the inclusive love of Christ in their daily lives.

Engaging with people from different backgrounds helps to break down stereotypes and prejudices that may unconsciously shape one's worldview. Through authentic interactions and shared experiences, individuals can challenge preconceived notions and develop a more nuanced understanding of others. This process fosters empathy by exposing individuals to the unique challenges and joys that others encounter, thereby broadening their perspective on what it means to love one's neighbor.

Building diverse friendships also enhances emotional intelligence and cultural sensitivity. As individuals navigate relationships with people from different walks of life, they develop skills in effective communication, active listening, and emotional support.

These skills are crucial for demonstrating Christian compassion, as they enable individuals to connect more deeply with others and offer genuine care and understanding.

Moreover, diverse relationships provide valuable opportunities for learning and growth. By engaging in conversations with individuals who have different life experiences, individuals gain insights into issues such as cultural heritage. This expanded knowledge helps individuals to advocate more effectively for vulnerable groups and contribute to efforts aimed at addressing social and economic disparities.

In addition, diverse friendships can inspire and motivate individuals to act in their communities. When individuals witness firsthand the resilience and strength of those facing adversity, they are often moved to contribute to positive change. This motivation can manifest in various forms, such as volunteering, supporting advocacy initiatives, or participating in community projects that address the needs of diverse populations.

Building diverse relationships also fosters a sense of solidarity and mutual support. By forming connections with people from different backgrounds, individuals create a network of allies and advocates who share a commitment to compassion and justice. This collective support strengthens efforts to promote inclusivity, reinforcing the Christian principle of loving one's neighbor and working towards the common good.

Furthermore, embracing diversity in relationships reflects the biblical vision of unity and inclusion. The Apostle Paul emphasizes in Galatians 3:28 that in Christ, there is neither Jew nor Gentile, neither slave nor free, neither male nor female, for all are one. By actively seeking and valuing relationships with individuals from various backgrounds, Christians live out this vision of unity and demonstrate the inclusive love of Christ in tangible ways.

Seeking diverse relationships is a crucial step in cultivating Christian compassion, as it broadens perspectives and deepens empathy. By building friendships with individuals from diverse backgrounds, individuals challenge stereotypes, enhance emotional intelligence, and gain valuable insights into social issues. These diverse connections inspire action, foster solidarity, and reflect the inclusive love of Christ, contributing to a more compassionate and just world. Through these relationships, individuals embody the essence of Christian love by embracing and supporting all people, honoring their unique experiences, and promoting unity within the community.

Reflecting On Personal Experiences

Reflecting on personal experiences of receiving compassion from others is a powerful motivator for extending the same kindness to those in need. These moments of compassion can deeply impact individuals, shaping their understanding of empathy and inspiring them to act with similar generosity. By revisiting these experiences, one can draw strength and motivation to cultivate a spirit of compassion in their own life.

One of the primary ways reflecting on personal experiences fosters compassion is by evoking a sense of gratitude. When individuals recall times when others have shown them kindness or support during challenging moments, they are reminded of the profound impact that compassion can have. This gratitude often translates into a desire to pay it forward, motivating individuals to offer support and care to others who may be experiencing hardship.

Moreover, personal experiences of receiving compassion often highlight the importance of connection and empathy. These moments reveal how meaningful and uplifting it can be to receive understanding and support from others. By reflecting on these experiences, individuals gain insight into the power of compassion to build relationships and alleviate suffering, reinforcing their commitment to extending similar care to those in need.

Reflecting on times of receiving compassion can also provide valuable lessons in how to effectively support others. For instance, one might recall specific actions or words that were particularly comforting or helpful during a difficult period. By remembering these details, individuals can apply similar approaches in their interactions, ensuring that their expressions of compassion are both thoughtful and impactful.

Additionally, personal experiences of compassion often reveal the importance of being present and attentive to others' needs. When individuals reflect on how they felt truly seen and heard during times of difficulty, they recognize the significance of offering that same level of presence and attention to others. This understanding encourages a more empathetic approach, where individuals actively listen and respond to the emotional and practical needs of those they seek to support.

Furthermore, reflecting on past instances of receiving compassion can deepen one's appreciation for the small, everyday acts of kindness that often go unnoticed. Whether it was a friend's reassuring words, a stranger's helping hand, or a family member's unwavering support, these seemingly minor gestures can leave a lasting impression. By acknowledging and valuing these acts, individuals are more likely to replicate them in their own lives, contributing to a culture of kindness and generosity.

Personal experiences of receiving compassion can also serve as a reminder of the shared human experience of vulnerability and need. Understanding that everyone, including oneself, has moments of struggle and requires support fosters a sense of solidarity. This recognition can motivate individuals to approach others with a greater sense of empathy and understanding, acknowledging that compassion is a universal need that transcends individual circumstances.

Finally, reflecting on personal experiences of compassion can strengthen one's commitment to living out Christian values. Jesus taught His followers to love their neighbors as themselves and to show compassion to the least among them. By recalling the ways they have been blessed by others' kindness, individuals can align their actions with these teachings, striving to embody Christ's love in their expressions of care and support.

Reflecting on personal experiences of receiving compassion is a transformative practice that enhances one's motivation to extend kindness to others. By recalling moments of support and empathy, individuals foster gratitude, gain insights into effective compassion, and deepen their understanding of the importance of connection and presence.

These reflections inspire individuals to replicate acts of kindness, appreciate everyday gestures, and strengthen their commitment to living out Christian values. Ultimately, this practice nurtures a compassionate spirit that seeks to make a positive difference in the lives of others, reflecting the love and care exemplified by Jesus Christ.

...for I was hungry and you gave me something to eat.
Matthew 25:35

8   *The CARE Ministry Model*

The CARE model consists of four basic components: compassion, acts of love, relationships, and evangelism. The four components are both interrelated and progressive. The model begins with compassion. Lasting and significant life-change comes because people in need know that believers truly care.

The second component in the CARE model is acts of love. The provision of needs is a critical aspect of compassion ministries, directly addressing the physical, emotional, and practical challenges that individuals face. Many people who come to compassion ministries are in crisis, struggling with basic needs such as food, shelter, clothing, and healthcare. By meeting these needs, ministries provide immediate relief and stability, which is often necessary before any other form of support can be effective.

Compassion, true Christian compassion, always leads one to move, to reach out, to take action. Compassion without action is not compassion. Acts of love are the natural result of compassion. When Jesus had compassion on someone, He touched them, He fed them, He healed them, or met some other need in their life. Luke records in Acts the story of Dorcas who was a woman of compassion.

> *In Joppa there was a disciple named Tabitha, which is trans-lated Dorcas. She was always doing good works and acts of charity.* Acts 9:36

Dorcas was a compassionate Christian who spent her days doing good works and acts of love.

Acts of love can meet physical, emotional, financial, educational, or other needs. Acts of love can be planned or spontaneous.

Some might ask if the CARE model's acts of love are the same as random acts of kindness. They point to the fact that kindness is one of the fruits of the Spirit. Though the actual acts may be similar, the two are not the same. Acts

Acts of love in the CARE model are directed to people in need: the poor, the homeless, and more.

of kindness can relate to anyone: a neighbor, a stranger, a friend. Someone offers to babysit without being paid so a couple can go out to dinner. You pay for the breakfast of the person who is behind you in the drive-up line. Acts of love in the CARE model are directed to people in need: the poor, the disenfranchised, the lonely, the homeless, the widow, the orphan, and others.

Acts of love are also different from most acts of kindness in that they are not random. They are targeted and intentional. The purpose of acts of love is also different from the purpose of most acts of kindness. Acts of kindness are designed to brighten someone's day. Acts of love are designed to change someone's life. Finally, acts of love are different from random acts of kindness as they seek to build long-term relationships with those in need. Most random acts of kindness are not normally designed to build lasting relationships.

The third component of the CARE model is relationships. Building relationships is at the very heart of effective compassionate care. In compassion ministries, the depth and quality of relationships often determine the impact and sustainability of the care provided. True compassion goes beyond meeting immediate needs; it involves connecting with people on a personal level, understanding their stories, and walking alongside them in their journey. This relational approach is what transforms charitable acts into meaningful, long-lasting support that can change lives.

Relationships in compassionate care are rooted in trust. Trust is essential because it allows those in need to feel safe and valued. Many individuals who seek help from compassion ministries have experienced trauma, rejection, or marginalization, making trust difficult to establish. Building trust requires consistency, honesty, and a genuine commitment to the well-being of others. When trust is established, it opens the door for deeper engagement and more effective ministry, as people are more likely to be open and responsive to support when they feel they can rely on those offering it.

The CARE Ministry Model

→ Me to volunteers

COMPASSIONATE HEARTS

Having a genuine concern for others. Driven by a desire to help those in need.

ACTS OF LOVE

Practical demonstrations of care. Meeting needs through acts of kindness.

RELATIONSHIPS

Building relationships based on trust and respect. Fostering genuine connections.

EVANGELISM

Opportunities to share the Gospel. Leading people to a saving knowledge of Jesus.

Empathy is another critical component of building relationships in compassionate care. To truly connect with others, ministry workers must strive to understand and share the feelings of those they serve. Empathy allows caregivers to step into the shoes of others, seeing the world from their perspective. This not only fosters a deeper connection but also informs more compassionate and appropriate responses to their needs. In this way, empathy moves compassionate care from a transactional act of charity to a relational act of love.

In addition to trust and empathy, mutual respect is vital in building relationships within compassion ministries. Respecting the dignity and autonomy of each person is crucial, as it acknowledges their worth and agency. This means recognizing and valuing their experiences, beliefs, and choices, even when they differ from our own. Mutual respect helps to create a partnership rather than a hierarchical relationship, where both parties feel empowered and engaged. When people feel respected, they are more likely to take an active role in their healing and growth, making the care provided more effective.

Consistency and commitment are also key in building lasting relationships in compassionate ministry. Relationships take time to develop, and they require ongoing effort and presence. Inconsistent or sporadic support can undermine trust and make individuals feel undervalued. However, when ministry workers show up consistently, demonstrating commitment to the long-term process, it reassures those in need that they are not alone and that the support will continue regardless of circumstances. This ongoing presence is a powerful expression of God's steadfast love.

Listening is a fundamental skill in relationship-building that is often overlooked. In compassionate care, listening is not just about hearing words but about understanding the heart behind them. Active listening involves giving full attention to the person speaking, acknowledging their feelings, and responding thoughtfully. This approach helps individuals feel truly heard and understood, which can be deeply healing in itself. Through listening, ministry workers can better discern the specific needs and hopes of those they serve, leading to more personalized and effective care.

Relational ministry also emphasizes the importance of community and belonging. Compassionate care should aim to integrate individuals into a supportive community where they can find ongoing encouragement and connection. The church or ministry itself can serve as this community, offering a safe space where people are accepted, loved, and valued. Relationships built within this community help combat the isolation that many in need often experience, fostering a sense of belonging and purpose that is crucial for long-term recovery and growth.

Mentorship and discipleship are powerful relational tools in compassion ministries. By pairing individuals with mentors who can guide, support, and encourage them, ministries create a structure for deep, personal relationships that can lead to significant transformation. Mentors provide not just practical advice but also spiritual guidance, helping individuals grow in their faith and navigate the challenges they face. The relational aspect of mentorship ensures that care is not only provided in the moment but continues as individuals journey toward healing and wholeness.

The reciprocal nature of relationships in compassionate care is also important to acknowledge. While those in need receive support, they often contribute to the lives of their caregivers in meaningful ways. Building relationships in ministry creates opportunities for mutual growth, where both parties learn, grow, and experience God's love through their interactions. This reciprocity enriches the ministry experience and reinforces the idea that everyone has something valuable to offer, regardless of their circumstances.

Building relationships through compassion ministries can also provide a good picture of a person's spiritual condition. Often through relationship building, a believer finds that the person in need is already a Christian. Fellowship then becomes an important aspect of the relationship. The common bond of faith provides the foundation for deep and significant sharing, comfort, and more. The sense of family and belonging that shared faith brings can be life-changing and lifesaving for those in need.

In the context of building a relationship, one may discover that the person in need is not a believer. In that case, the relationship can provide valuable information regarding the person's views of God, past religious experiences, and more.

Building relationships through compassion ministries also gives those in need a picture of the relationship that God desires to have with them in Christ. The nurture and care provided by the believer is what the Father offers in a relationship with Him. Those in need can also see the relationship that the believer has with Christ and the difference the Savior can make in their own life. Observing the life of a growing, caring Christian has led many to the Lord.

> *Sharing God's love makes people aware of their need for God's love in Christ.*

The fourth component of the CARE model is evangelism. Relationships built through effective compassion ministries can lead to an open door for evangelism. As stated earlier, evangelism is not the primary motive for compassion ministries. Believers meet needs because the love of God lives within their hearts. Also, as discussed earlier, meeting needs is not evangelism. Evangelism is sharing the message of salvation in Christ through a verbal witness based on Scripture. Service and evangelism are two separate functions of the church. The evangelism strategy of a church should not be limited to evangelism that happens as a result of providing compassion ministries. Members should be involved in personal evangelism through relationships they have outside service ministries.

Service through compassion ministries can, however, lead to evangelism. Sharing God's love makes people aware of their need for God's love in Christ. As believers communicate their Christian compassion, meet needs, build relationships, and share their own journeys of faith, non-believers are often receptive to the gospel. A more detailed discussion of the role of evangelism and a model for evangelism is provided in Chapter 11.

The CARE ministry model, therefore, is not a prescribed set of programs. CARE is a template from which a ministry, under the leadership of the Holy Spirit, can design a strategy that is tailored to its particular setting and resources. Through compassion, acts of love, relationships, and evangelism, the ministry is used by God to meet needs and share Christ. When those connections are made, lives are changed.

Your kingdom come. Your will be done
...thy will be done on earth as it is in heaven.
Matthew 6:10

9   Creating a Culture of Compassion

Creating a culture of compassion within a church is essential for fostering a community that reflects the love and grace of Christ. A compassionate church is one that actively engages in meeting the needs of its community, embodying the teachings of Jesus in practical, tangible ways.

To cultivate such a culture, churches must be intentional in encouraging compassion among their members. This chapter explores practical ways to nurture compassion within a church, ensuring that it becomes an integral part of the church's identity and mission.

Teaching And Preaching On Compassion

One of the most effective ways to encourage compassion among church members is through consistent teaching and preaching on the biblical foundations of compassion. Church leaders play a crucial role in shaping the values and priorities of the congregation, and regularly addressing the theme of compassion in sermons, Bible studies, and small groups can inspire members to embrace this essential Christian virtue.

Preaching and teaching should highlight the numerous examples of compassion found in the Bible, such as the Good Samaritan, Jesus' healing of the sick and feeding of the hungry, and the early church's care for the poor (Acts 2:44-45). By connecting these stories to the lives of the congregation, church leaders can demonstrate how compassion is not just a historical concept but a living, active expression of faith.

Sermons and lessons should not only teach about compassion but also provide practical applications. For example, a sermon on the Good Samaritan could be followed by a challenge for members to identify and respond to needs in their own community. Providing specific, actionable steps helps to bridge the gap between belief and practice, making it easier for members to live out compassion in their daily lives.

Modeling Compassionate Leadership

Church leaders must model the compassion they wish to see in their congregation. When members see their pastors, elders, and ministry leaders actively engaging in compassionate acts such as visiting the sick, supporting the grieving, or advocating for the vulnerable, they are more likely to follow suit.

Leaders should be visibly involved in compassion ministries, whether that's serving in a food pantry, leading a mission trip, or offering pastoral care to those in need. When leaders prioritize compassion in their own lives, it sets a powerful example for the congregation and reinforces the message that compassion is central to the church's mission.

Leaders should also foster a servant leadership mentality among other church members. This involves empowering others to take on leadership roles in compassion ministries and recognizing that every member of the church has a role to play in serving others. By decentralizing leadership and by encouraging broad participation, a church can create a culture where compassion is everyone's responsibility.

Providing Opportunities For Compassionate Service

Creating a culture of compassion requires providing church members with ample opportunities to practice compassion. This involves organizing and promoting ministries and initiatives that focus on meeting the needs of others, both within the church and in the wider community.

Churches can organize local outreach programs that allow members to serve their community in practical ways. Examples include food drives, community clean-up days, visiting nursing homes, or providing support for homeless shelters. These activities not only meet immediate needs but also help to build relationships between church members and those they serve, fostering a deeper understanding of the challenges faced by others.

Mission trips, whether local or international, provide church members with opportunities to serve in new contexts and witness the impact of compassion on a larger scale. Service projects, such as building homes, providing medical care, or teaching skills, allow members to use their talents in service to others, reinforcing the importance of compassion in the Christian life.

Churches should also provide opportunities for members to serve one another. This could include organizing meals for families in crisis, offering transportation for the elderly, or providing childcare for single parents. By serving each other within the church, members can practice compassion in a supportive environment and develop a habit of looking out for the needs of others.

Celebrating Acts of Compassion

Recognizing and celebrating acts of compassion within the church reinforces their importance and encourages others to follow suit. When members see that compassionate actions are valued and appreciated, they are more likely to engage in similar behaviors.

Churches can publicly recognize acts of compassion during services or in church communications, such as newsletters or social media. Highlighting stories of members who have gone out of their way to help others serves as an inspiration to the entire congregation and creates a culture where compassion is celebrated.

Some churches establish annual awards or celebrations to honor those who have demonstrated exceptional compassion in their service to others. These events not only recognize individuals but also bring the congregation together to celebrate the impact of compassionate ministry on the church and the community.

Integrating Compassion Into Church Life

Finally, a culture of compassion is most effectively created when it is integrated into all aspects of church life. This involves ensuring that compassion is a core value in every ministry, program, and activity within the church.

Churches can make compassion one of their core values, integrating it into their mission statement, goals, and strategic plans. When compassion is one of the church's foundational values, it naturally influences decisions, priorities, and even behaviors.

> *Churches can make compassion one of their core values, integrating it into their mission statement.*

Worship services can regularly include prayers for compassion, reflections on compassionate scriptures, and sermons that challenge members to live out their faith through acts of love. By making compassion a regular theme in worship, churches keep it at the forefront of their collective consciousness.

Creating a culture of compassion within the church requires intentionality, leadership, and practical action. By teaching and modeling compassion, providing opportunities for service, encouraging reflection, celebrating acts of love, and integrating compassion into all aspects of church life, churches can foster a community that truly reflects the heart of Christ. As members grow in their commitment to compassion, they will not only transform their own lives but also make a profound impact on the lives of others, both within the church and in the wider world.

Whoever is generous to the poor lends to the Lord.
Proverbs 19:17

10   Ministry Assessments and Plans

To implement effective compassion ministries churches must adopt strategies that are both intentional and sustainable. This chapter explores three key components for implementing compassion ministries: assessing church ministry capacity, assessing community needs, and strategic planning.

Assessing Church Ministry Capacity

Assessing a church's capacity for compassion ministry is a critical step in ensuring that the church can effectively meet the needs of its members and the surrounding community. This process involves evaluating the church's resources, strengths, and potential challenges, as well as identifying areas for growth and improvement. A thorough assessment allows church leaders to make informed decisions about how to best utilize their resources and develop strategies for sustainable and impactful ministry.

The first step in assessing a church's capacity for compassion ministry is to take stock of the resources and strengths that the church already possesses. This includes both tangible resources, such as finances and facilities, and intangible resources, such as volunteer availability, skills, and spiritual gifts.

A church's financial health plays a significant role in determining the scale and scope of its compassion ministry. Assessing financial resources involves reviewing the church's budget to determine how much can be allocated to compassion initiatives. This includes not only direct funding for programs but also indirect costs such as staff salaries, facility maintenance, and administrative expenses.

The church's physical resources, including its building, vehicles, and equipment, are crucial in determining its capacity to host and facilitate compassion ministry activities. For example, a church with a large kitchen and dining area may be well-suited to operate a community meal program, while a church with transportation resources might be able to offer rides to medical appointments or job interviews.

Volunteers are the lifeblood of most compassion ministries. Assessing the availability and engagement of volunteers within the congregation is essential to understanding the church's capacity to sustain and grow its ministry efforts. This assessment should consider the number of active volunteers, their skill sets, and their willingness to commit time and energy to compassion initiatives.

In addition to volunteer availability, it is important to assess the specific skills and spiritual gifts present within the congregation.

For example, members with skills in counseling, healthcare, education, or construction can be invaluable in specialized compassion ministries. Similarly, spiritual gifts such as mercy, service, and hospitality are particularly relevant to compassion work. Understanding the unique talents within the church can help tailor ministries to maximize impact.

While it's important to recognize a church's strengths, it is equally important to identify potential challenges and limitations that could affect its capacity for compassion ministry. Being aware of these challenges allows church leaders to develop strategies to mitigate or overcome them.

Many churches face financial constraints that limit their ability to fund compassion ministries. If financial resources are limited, it may be necessary to prioritize certain initiatives over others or seek alternative funding sources such as grants, donations, or partnerships with other organizations.

One of the common challenges in compassion ministry is the risk of volunteer burnout. If a small group of volunteers is shouldering the majority of the work, they may become overwhelmed, leading to fatigue and disengagement. Assessing volunteer engagement levels and ensuring that the workload is distributed equitably is key to sustaining volunteer enthusiasm and preventing burnout.

Effective compassion ministry requires strong leadership to coordinate efforts, motivate volunteers, and manage resources. Assessing the leadership capacity within the church includes evaluating the availability of leaders who are enthusiastic about compassion ministry and have the necessary skills to guide and grow these efforts. If leadership capacity is lacking, it may be necessary to invest in leadership development or recruit additional leaders.

For compassion ministry to thrive, it needs broad support and commitment from the congregation. Assessing the level of congregational buy-in involves determining the congregation's interest in and commitment to compassion

> *For compassion ministry to thrive, it needs broad support and commitment from the congregation*

ministry. If interest is low, church leaders may need to invest in education and awareness campaigns to build enthusiasm and support for these efforts.

Assessing a church's capacity for compassion ministry is a vital step in ensuring that the church can effectively meet the needs of the community. By evaluating resources, strengths, challenges, and opportunities for growth, church leaders can move to the next step of assessing community needs. A CHURCH ASSESSMENT IS PROVIDED AT THE END OF THE BOOK.

Assessing Community Needs

One of the most crucial steps in implementing compassionate practices is understanding the specific needs of the community. Without a clear understanding of these needs, efforts may be misdirected or ineffective. Therefore, conducting thorough community assessments and tailoring ministry efforts to address identified issues are essential strategies.

A community assessment is a systematic process of gathering information about the community's needs, resources, and challenges. This process helps church leaders and members understand the context in which they are ministering and allows them to tailor their efforts to meet real and pressing needs.

One effective method for conducting a community assessment is through surveys and interviews with community members. These tools can help gather insights into the specific challenges faced by different groups, such as families, the elderly, or those experiencing homelessness. By directly engaging with the community, churches can gain a deeper understanding of the most pressing issues and the best ways to address them.

Collaborating with local organizations, such as schools, social services, and nonprofits, can also provide valuable data and insights. These organizations often have a wealth of information about the community's needs and can help identify gaps that the church might address. Building these partnerships also opens doors for collaboration and resource sharing, enhancing the church's ability to meet community needs.

Once the needs of the community have been identified, the next step is to tailor the church's compassion ministry to address these specific issues. Tailoring efforts ensures that the ministry is relevant and impactful.

Based on the findings of the community assessment, churches can develop focused programs that directly address the identified needs. For example, if food insecurity is a significant issue, the church might establish a food pantry or meal distribution program. If mental health is a concern, the church could offer counseling services or support groups. By aligning ministry efforts with community needs, the church can make a meaningful difference in the lives of those it serves.

It is important to remain flexible and adaptive in ministry approaches. As community needs evolve, so too should the church's efforts. Regularly revisiting and updating the community assessment helps ensure that the ministry remains relevant and responsive to current issues.

Strategic Planning

Based on the church and community assessments, church leaders can develop a strategic plan for compassion ministry that aligns with the church's assets and the community's needs. This plan should include specific, measurable goals, such as increasing the number of volunteers, expanding services, or launching new initiatives. A clear plan provides direction and helps ensure that resources are used effectively.

To enhance the church's capacity for compassion ministry, it may be necessary to invest in capacity-building initiatives. This could include training programs for volunteers and leaders, upgrading facilities, or developing new partnerships with other churches and organizations. By building capacity, the church can increase its ability to serve and make a greater impact in the community.

Partnerships with other churches, nonprofits, and community organizations can significantly enhance a church's capacity for compassion ministry. These partnerships allow for resource sharing, collaboration on projects, and access to expertise that may not be available within the church itself. Assessing the potential for partnerships can open new avenues for ministry and increase the church's overall impact.

Finally, it's important to recognize that assessing a church's capacity for compassion ministry is not a one-time event but an ongoing process. Regular assessments allow the church to adapt to changing circumstances, address emerging needs, and continuously improve its ministry efforts. This iterative process ensures that the church remains responsive to the community and effective in its mission.

Sustaining compassion ministry over the long term requires intentional strategies to maintain momentum and ensure that efforts remain impactful and relevant. Long-term sustainability is a common challenge in compassion ministry, particularly as initial enthusiasm may wane over time. To maintain momentum, churches must be proactive in their planning and execution. Periodically evaluating the effectiveness of compassion ministry initiatives helps ensure that they continue to meet community needs and engage volunteers.

Gathering feedback from those being served and from volunteers can provide valuable insights into what's working well and what needs improvement. Based on this feedback, churches can adapt their programs to better serve the community and keep participants motivated.

Implementing compassionate ministries requires intentional strategies that are both practical and sustainable. By identifying and meeting community needs through thorough assessments and tailored ministry efforts, empowering individuals to participate through training and encouragement, and sustaining momentum through regular evaluation and spiritual disciplines, churches can build a robust and enduring culture of compassion ministry. These strategies not only enhance the church's ability to serve effectively but also help create a community that truly reflects the love and care of Christ in the world.

Go into all the world and preach the gospel.
Mark 16:15

11   Evangelism and Compassion Ministry

Evangelism and compassion are two vital aspects of Christian ministry that, when combined, create a powerful and holistic approach to sharing the gospel. Compassion opens hearts and builds trust, creating opportunities to communicate the message of Christ in a way that is genuine and impactful. Here we explore the connection between compassion and evangelism and practical approaches to integrating evangelism into compassion ministry.

The Connection Between Compassion and Evangelism

Compassion and evangelism are deeply intertwined in the Christian faith. Compassion, as a tangible expression of love, often serves as a bridge to evangelism by opening doors for meaningful conversations about faith. When people experience the love of Christ through acts of compassion, they become more receptive to hearing about the gospel message.

Acts of compassion can soften hearts and break down barriers that might otherwise prevent people from being open to the message of Christ. Compassionate actions demonstrate the love of God in a tangible way, making the gospel more accessible and relatable. When people see that Christians genuinely care about their well-being, both physically and spiritually, they are more likely to be open to hearing about the source of that love.

For example, when a church provides food and shelter to those in need, it is not only meeting immediate physical needs but also showing the love of Christ in action. This practical demonstration of compassion can lead to conversations about why the

> *A practical demonstration of compassion can open the door for discussions about Jesus and the message of salvation.*

church is motivated to help, opening the door for discussions about Jesus and His message of salvation. In this way, compassion serves as a precursor to evangelism, preparing the ground for the seed of the gospel to be planted.

Integrating evangelism into compassion ministry requires intentionality and sensitivity. It is essential to approach evangelism in a way that respects the dignity and autonomy of those being served, ensuring that the message of Christ is communicated with love and humility.

One effective technique for integrating evangelism into compassion ministry is through relational evangelism as outlined earlier in the CARE Ministry Model. This approach focuses on building genuine relationships with those being served, creating a foundation of trust and respect. As relationships deepen, natural opportunities arise to share the gospel in a way that is relevant and meaningful to the individual. Relational evangelism emphasizes listening, understanding the person's story, and sharing the message of Christ in a way that speaks to their specific context and needs.

Another approach is to offer prayer as part of compassion ministry. For example, when providing food or other assistance, volunteers can offer to pray with or for the individuals they are serving. This simple gesture can open the door to spiritual conversations and provide a natural transition to sharing the gospel. Offering prayer demonstrates care for the person's spiritual needs and can lead to opportunities for further discussion about faith.

Churches can also incorporate evangelistic materials, such as Bibles, tracts, or other Christian literature, into their compassion efforts. However, it is important to do so in a way that is non-coercive and respectful. Providing these resources as an option, rather than a requirement, allows individuals to engage with the gospel message at their own pace.

When sharing faith within the context of service, it is crucial to prioritize the dignity and autonomy of those being served. Evangelism should never feel like an obligation or a condition for receiving help. Instead, it should be offered as an expression of love and concern for the person's holistic well-being.

One way to ensure that evangelism is conducted respectfully is by focusing on the person's needs and interests rather than pushing an agenda. Listening to their story, understanding their struggles, and responding with empathy creates an environment where the message of Christ can be shared naturally and meaningfully.

Another key principle is to avoid any form of manipulation or coercion. The gospel should be presented as an invitation rather than a demand, allowing individuals to explore and respond to the message in their own time. This approach respects their freedom and ensures that any decision to follow Christ is made genuinely and voluntarily.

Stories of lives transformed through compassionate evangelism illustrate the powerful impact that this approach can have. These testimonies serve as a reminder of how acts of love and service can lead to spiritual breakthroughs and lasting change.

One compelling example is the story of a man named Tom, who was struggling with homelessness and addiction. A local church began offering meals and shelter to those in need, and Tom started attending regularly. The church members not only provided for his physical needs but also took the time to build a relationship with him, offering consistent support and encouragement. Over time, Tom began to open up about his struggles, and through the care and compassion he received, he became receptive to hearing about the gospel. One evening, after a meaningful conversation, Tom decided to give his life to Christ. Today, he is sober, has a stable job, and serves in the same ministry that helped him find hope.

Another example is the story of Maria, a single mother who was overwhelmed with the challenges of raising her children alone. A group of women from a local church started visiting her regularly, offering help with childcare, groceries, and household chores. Through their ongoing support, Maria experienced the love of Christ in a tangible way. Their consistent acts of kindness and their willingness to listen and pray with her opened her heart to the gospel. Eventually, Maria accepted an invitation to attend a church service, where she heard the gospel message and chose to follow Christ. Her life was transformed, and she now actively participates in the church, helping other women who are in similar situations.

These stories highlight several important lessons for effectively combining compassion with evangelism. First, they demonstrate the importance of building genuine relationships. Compassionate evangelism is most effective when it is rooted in a sincere concern for the individual, not just as a target for conversion but as a person deserving of love and respect.

Second, these testimonies underscore the need for patience and persistence. Transformation often takes time, and it is essential to remain committed to serving and supporting individuals even when there are no immediate results. Compassionate evangelism is about sowing seeds of love and truth, trusting that God will bring the harvest in His time.

Finally, these stories emphasize the importance of living out our faith. Acts of compassion create credibility and provide a powerful witness to the truth of the gospel. When people see the love of Christ demonstrated in practical ways, they are more likely to be open to hearing about the source of that love.

Evangelism in the CARE ministry model presented earlier is framed by four basic components: compassion, discernment, presentation, and invitation. Believers must be as passionate about evangelism as they are about meeting physical, emotional, financial, or other needs. When Jesus wept over the city of Jerusalem, He was weeping about their spiritual condition. They were like sheep without a shepherd. Believers must have a genuine concern for the spiritual needs of those they minister to through compassion ministries. Going through the steps of an evangelistic program without compassion rarely produces fruit.

The second component of the CARE evangelism strategy is discernment. Believers must pray and seek God's guidance when preparing to share the gospel. Timing is often an issue. Some would boldly proclaim that the right time to share the gospel is right now. Most would agree that there is an urgency about sharing the gospel but many, if not most, would also agree that discernment is needed with regard to a person's level of understanding and receptivity.

In the CARE model, believers rely on the leading of the Holy Spirit regarding the timing of a gospel presentation. Discernment is also needed with regard to the manner in which the gospel is shared. Believers should search for ways to share the gospel that are understandable and relevant to the person's life.

The third component of the CARE evangelism model is presentation. Evangelism is not evangelism if the gospel is not shared. Believers must be trained and prepared to share the message of Jesus. The gospel presentation should include the fact that God loves the individual, Jesus came to show God's love, every person in the world is a sinner who has rejected God's love and God's rule in their life, sin carries a penalty that the sinner cannot pay, Jesus paid for sin on the cross, salvation comes by accepting Christ as Savior and Lord.

The fourth component of the CARE evangelistic model is invitation. Compassion motivates the believer to engage. Discernment helps the believer to know when and how to share the gospel. Presentation lays out God's plan of redemption. Invitation is an offer to experience new life in Christ. The invitation may be rejected or accepted but it is the responsibility of Christians to invite non-believers to accept Christ as Savior. If a decision for Christ is not made, the believer's compassion should not be quenched. Additional prayer, continuing the relationship, and presenting the gospel again may eventually lead to a decision for Christ.

Evangelism through compassion is a powerful approach to sharing the gospel. Acts of compassion open doors for meaningful conversations about faith, demonstrating the love of Christ in action. By integrating evangelism into compassion ministry through relational approaches, respectful communication, and consistent acts of service, churches can effectively reach people with the message of Christ. Through compassionate evangelism, the church fulfills its mission to make disciples while embodying the heart of Christ in the world.

Chapter Sources

Chapter 1

Walton, John H. "The Role of Compassion in the Abrahamic Narrative of Genesis." *Biblical Interpretation Journal*, vol. 12, no. 3, 2004, pp. 315-331.

Berlin, Adele. "Divine Compassion in the Old Testament: A Study of Genesis." *Journal for the Study of the Old Testament*, vol. 20, no. 1, 1995, pp. 23-41.

Crenshaw, James L. *The Compassion of the Father: A Study of Divine Empathy in the Old Testament*. Yale University Press, 2001.

Stone, Bryan. *Compassionate Ministry: Theological Foundations*. Orbis Books, Maryknoll, NY, 1996

Chapter 2

Davies, W. D. "The Compassionate God of the Old Testament." *Journal of Theological Studies* 52, no. 2 (2001): 173-198.

Janzen, J. Gerald. *The Character of God in the Book of Genesis: A Narrative Appraisal*. Louisville: Westminster John Knox Press, 2009.

Stone, Bryan. *Compassionate Ministry: Theological Foundations*. Orbis Books, Maryknoll, NY, 1996

Wright, Christopher J. H. *The Mission of God: Unlocking the Bible's Grand Narrative.* Downers Grove, IL: InterVarsity Press, 2006.

Harris, R. Laird. *Exploring the Love of God.* Nashville: Thomas Nelson, 2011.

Levenson, Jon D. *The Love of God: Divine Gift, Human Gratitude, and Mutual Faithfulness in Judaism.* Princeton: Princeton University Press, 2016.

David H. Englehart. "Compassion", *Baker's Evangelical Dictionary of Biblical Theology*, Web. www.biblestudytools.com

D. A. Bayliss, *Compassion.* Web. http://www.adbhand.org/ Word%20Studies/Compassion.htm

Jim Myers, "Hesed: Mercy or Loyalty?", Biblical Heritage Center. Web. http://www.biblicalheritage.org/bible%20stud ies/hesed.htm

Chapter 3

Davies, W. D. "The Compassionate God of the Old Testament." *Journal of Theological Studies* 52, no. 2 (2001): 173-198.

Fretheim, Terence E. *God and World in the Old Testament: A Relational Theology of Creation.* Nashville: Abingdon Press, 2005.

Janzen, J. Gerald. *The Character of God in the Book of Genesis: A Narrative Appraisal.* Louisville: Westminster John Knox Press, 2009.

Wright, Christopher J. H. *The Mission of God: Unlocking the Bible's Grand Narrative*. Downers Grove, IL: InterVarsity Press, 2006.

Boda, Mark J. "Mercy in the Pentateuch: A Theological Exploration." *Catholic Biblical Quarterly* 66, no. 1 (2004): 1-14.

Carroll R., M. Daniel. "Amos and the Theology of Compassion." *Journal for the Study of the Old Testament* 28, no. 4 (2004): 435-448.

Fischer, Irmtraud. "Compassion and Lamentation in the Book of Lamentations." *Biblical Theology Bulletin* 34, no. 2 (2004): 82-93.

Hays, Christopher B. "Compassion in the Prophets: A Case Study in Micah." *Journal for the Study of the Old Testament* 30, no. 4 (2006): 443-458.

Chapter 4

Allison, Dale C. "Jesus' Compassion in the Gospel Tradition: A Comparative Analysis." *Journal of Biblical Literature* 121, no. 4 (2002): 563-583.

Crossan, John Dominic. "Jesus' Compassionate Ministry in Historical Perspective." *Journal for the Study of the Historical Jesus* 4, no. 1 (2006): 49-71.

Davies, W. D. "The Compassionate Jesus in the Synoptic Gospels." *New Testament Studies* 47, no. 2 (2001): 123-139.

Hagner, Donald A. "The Compassion of Jesus in the Gospel of Matthew." *Expository Times* 114, no. 8 (2003): 257-264.

Hooker, Morna D. "Compassion and Power: The Ministry of Jesus in Mark's Gospel." *Journal of Biblical Literature* 125, no. 2 (2006): 317-335.

Keener, Craig S. "The Compassionate Jesus in the Gospel of John." *Interpretation* 58, no. 3 (2004): 276-289.

McKnight, Scot. "Compassion and Forgiveness in the Parables of Jesus." *Journal for the Study of the Historical Jesus* 3, no. 2 (2005): 23-40.

Pennington, Jonathan T. "Compassionate Jesus: Exploring the Theme of Mercy in Matthew's Gospel." *Journal of Biblical Literature* 127, no. 4 (2008): 599-620.

Schweizer, Eduard. "The Compassionate Jesus: An Exegetical Study of the Gospels." *Journal for the Study of the New Testament* 28, no. 1 (2006): 3-20.

Stone, Bryan. *Compassionate Ministry: Theological Foundations.* Orbis Books, Maryknoll, NY, 1996

Wright, N. T. "Jesus' Compassion and the Kingdom of God in the Synoptic Gospels." *Journal for the Study of the Historical Jesus* 4, no. 1 (2006): 49-71.

Bayliss, D.A. *Compassion.* Web. http://www.adbhand.org/ Word%20Studies/Compassion.htm

Evans, Craig A. *The Compassionate Christ: A Socio-Historical Exploration of the Life and Teachings of Jesus.* Nashville: Abingdon Press, 2007.

Matera, Frank J. *The Passion Narratives and the Compassion of Jesus.* Grand Rapids: Eerdmans, 2004.

Chapter 5

Carson, D. A. *The Difficult Doctrine of the Love of God.* Wheaton, IL: Crossway, 2000.

Hays, Richard B. *The Moral Vision of the New Testament: Community, Cross, New Creation; A Contemporary Introduction to New Testament Ethics.* 2nd ed. New York: HarperOne, 2013.

Malina, Bruce J. "Social Science Commentary on the Compassionate Practices in the New Testament." *Biblical Theology Bulletin* 34, no. 4 (2004): 155-172.

Matera, Frank J. "The Ethics of Compassion in the Letters of Paul." *Interpretation* 59, no. 2 (2005): 127-138.

Rowe, C. Kavin. "The Compassionate God in the Acts of the Apostles." *Harvard Theological Review* 98, no. 4 (2005): 399-418.

Schweizer, Eduard. "Compassion in the Epistles: Pauline Perspectives on Mercy." *New Testament Studies* 49, no. 3 (2003): 241-258.

Thielman, Frank. "Compassionate Servanthood: The Example of Jesus in Philippians 2." *Journal for the Study of the New Testament* 28, no. 3 (2006): 259-276.

Chapter 6

Campbell, Heidi A. *Understanding Christian Compassion: A Handbook for Developing a Compassionate Heart.* Grand Rapids: Baker Academic, 2004.

Bass, Dorothy C. "Practicing Compassion: A Christian Tradition Revisited." *Journal of Religious Ethics* 31, no. 1 (2003): 99-117.

Beck, Richard. "The Heart of Compassion: Christian Perspectives on Emotional and Moral Development." *Journal of Psychology and Theology* 34, no. 1 (2006): 38-48.

Campbell, Heidi A. "Cultivating Compassionate Hearts: The Role of Christian Formation in Developing Emotional and Moral Resilience." *Theological Studies* 64, no. 3 (2007): 267-284.

Clough, David. "Learning Compassion: The Role of Christian Discipleship in Cultivating Compassionate Hearts." *Studies in Christian Ethics* 20, no. 2 (2007): 202-219.

Powell, Mark Allan. "Compassion as a Christian Virtue: Developing Emotional and Ethical Capacity through Spiritual Disciplines." *Journal of Theological Interpretation* 2, no. 2 (2008): 203-221.

Willard, Dallas. "Cultivating a Heart of Compassion: The Role of Spiritual Disciplines in Christian Life." *Christian Century* 121, no. 4 (2004): 10-17.

Wright, N. T. "Compassion and Christian Discipleship: The Transformation of the Heart in New Testament Contexts." *Journal for the Study of the New Testament* 29, no. 2 (2007): 177-196.

Chapter 7

Hancock, Aubrey Perry. *The Compassionate Church: Biblical, Missional, Transformational*, Aubrey Perry Hancock, 2015.

Chapter 8

Bass, Diana Butler. *Christianity for the Rest of Us: How the Neighborhood Church is Transforming the Faith.* New York: HarperOne, 2006.

Haugk, Kenneth C. *Christian Caregiving: A Way of Life.* Minneapolis: Augsburg Fortress, 2002.

Linthicum, Robert C. *Building a People of Power: Equipping Churches to Transform Their Communities.* Waynesboro, GA: Authentic Media, 2006.

McNeal, Reggie. *Missional Renaissance: Changing the Scorecard for the Church.* San Francisco: Jossey-Bass, 2009.

Nouwen, Henri J. M., Donald P. McNeill, and Douglas A. Morrison. *Compassion: A Reflection on the Christian Life.* New York: Image Books, 2005.

Snyder, Howard A., and Daniel V. Runyon. *Decoding the Church: Mapping the DNA of Christ's Body.* Grand Rapids: Baker Books, 2002.

Bass, Dorothy C. "Practicing Compassion: A Christian Tradition Revisited." *Journal of Religious Ethics* 31, no. 1 (2003): 99-117.

Beck, Richard. "The Heart of Compassion: Christian Perspectives on Emotional and Moral Development." *Journal of Psychology and Theology* 34, no. 1 (2006): 38-48.

Blumhofer, Edith L. "Creating a Culture of Compassion: Historical Perspectives on Church and Community Engagement." *Fides et Historia* 36, no. 2 (2004): 23-39.

Campbell, Heidi A. "Cultivating Compassionate Hearts: The Role of Christian Formation in Developing Emotional and Moral Resilience." *Theological Studies* 64, no. 3 (2007): 267-284.

Clough, David. "Learning Compassion: The Role of Christian Discipleship in Cultivating Compassionate Hearts." *Studies in Christian Ethics* 20, no. 2 (2007): 202-219.

Powell, Mark Allan. "Compassion as a Christian Virtue: Developing Emotional and Ethical Capacity through Spiritual Disciplines." *Journal of Theological Interpretation* 2, no. 2 (2008): 203-221.

Tisby, Jemar. "Creating a Culture of Compassion in the Local Church: The Role of Leadership and Community." *Review & Expositor* 108, no. 2 (2011): 223-239.

Willard, Dallas. "Cultivating a Heart of Compassion: The Role of Spiritual Disciplines in Christian Life." *Christian Century* 121, no. 4 (2004): 10-17.

Wright, N. T. "Compassion and Christian Discipleship: The Transformation of the Heart in New Testament Contexts." *Journal for the Study of the New Testament* 29, no. 2 (2007): 177-196.

Chapter 9

Ammerman, Nancy T. "Congregational Assessment: Understanding Congregational Identity in a Changing World." *Review of Religious Research* 45, no. 3 (2004): 251-269.

Bass, Dorothy C. "Assessing Community Needs for Effective Compassion Ministry." *Journal of Religious Leadership* 2, no. 2 (2003): 1-18.

Carroll, Jackson W. "Community Assessment and Congregational Leadership." *Journal of Pastoral Care & Counseling* 59, no. 3 (2005): 201-216.

Chaves, Mark. "Congregations' Impact on Local Communities: Assessing Church-Based Social Capital." *Sociology of Religion* 63, no. 4 (2002): 393-417.

Fuder, John. "Urban Ministry and Community Assessment: A Theological Perspective." *Journal of Urban Mission* 5, no. 2 (2006): 101-117.

Linthicum, Robert C. "Building Community: A Biblical Perspective on Church and Community Assessment." *Journal of Urban Theology* 4, no. 1 (2001): 5-22.

Roxburgh, Alan J. "Creating Missional Churches: Community Assessment as a Tool for Congregational Change." *Journal of Missional Practice* 3, no. 1 (2010): 57-68.

Stetzer, Ed. "The Role of Church Assessment in Effective Ministry Planning." *The Journal of Applied Christian Leadership* 4, no. 1 (2010): 19-28.

Swinton, John. "Assessing Compassion Ministry in Congregational Settings: Theological and Practical Implications." *Practical Theology* 5, no. 2 (2012): 145-160.

Chapter 10

Stephen Curtis Chapman, "What Now." Audio CD, All Things New, Sparrow, 2004.

Chapter 11

Green, Michael. *Evangelism in the Early Church*. Grand Rapids, Michigan: Wm. B. Eerdmans Publishing, 2004.

Kinnaman, David. *unChristian: What a New Generation Really Thinks About Christianity ... And Why It Matters*. Grand Rapids, Michigan: Baker Books, 2007.

Stetzer, Ed, and Im, Daniel. *Planting Missional Churches: Your Guide to Starting Churches that Multiply*. B&H Academic, 2016.

Stetzer, Ed, and Rainer, Thom S. *Transformational Church: Creating a New Scorecard for Congregations*. B&H Books, 2010.

Stone, Bryan. *Compassionate Ministry: Theological Foundations*. Orbis Books, Maryknoll, NY, 1996

Additional Resources

The listing of a resource does not constitute an endorsement of the author's theological, political, or social views.

What Every Church Member Should Know about Poverty by Bill Ehlig and Ruby K. Payne

When Helping Hurts: How to Alleviate Poverty Without Hurting the Poor and Yourself by Steve Corbett, Brian Fikkert

Toxic Charity: How Churches and Charities Hurt Those They Help (And How to Reverse It) by Robert D. Lupton

Meeting Needs Sharing Christ by Donald A. Atkinson and Charles L. Roesel

The Compassionate Congregation: A Handbook for People Who Care by Karen Mulder and Ginger Jurries

The Hole in Our Gospel: What Does God Expect of Us? The Answer That Changed My Life and Might Just Change the World by Richard Stearns

Fast Living: How The Church Will End Extreme Poverty by Scott C. Todd PhD

The Unlikely Missionary: From Pew-Warmer to Poverty-Fighter by Dan King and Tom Davis

Seeing Children Seeing God: A Practical Theology of Children and Poverty by Pamela Couture

Barefoot Church: Serving the Least in a Consumer Culture by Brandon Hatmaker

The Invisible: What the Church Can Do to Find and Serve the Least of These by Arloa Sutter

The Poor Will Be Glad: Joining the Revolution to Lift the World Out of Poverty by Peter Greer and Phil Smith

Compassion Evangelism: Meeting Human Needs by Thomas G. Nees

Disrupting Homelessness: Alternative Christian Approaches by Laura Stivers

Together ALL USA Churches and Christians CAN END USA Homelessness by Rev John Sobiech

Thrift Store Saints: Meeting Jesus 25 Cents at a Time by Jane Knuth

My 30 Days Under the Overpass: Not Your Ordinary Devotional by Mike Yankoski

Ending Poverty: A 20/20 Vision: A Guide for Individuals and Congregations by Nancy Maeker

Rich Thinking About the World's Poor: Seeing Poverty Through God's Eyes by Peter Meadows

Article - Developing A Support Ministry For Women Experiencing Generational Poverty

Introduction

Generational poverty, characterized by cycles of economic hardship spanning several decades, presents profound challenges that extend far beyond financial constraints. For women caught in its grasp, the journey is marked by a painful social stigma, low self-esteem, and emotional burdens that weigh heavily on their hearts and minds.

Ministering to women who have experienced generational poverty is more than just providing material aid or temporary relief. It is a sacred commitment to walk alongside them on their journey toward healing, resilience, and renewal. It is about creating spaces of sanctuary where their voices are heard, their experiences are validated, and their aspirations are honored. It is about cultivating a culture of compassion and empathy that recognizes the inherent worth and dignity of every individual, regardless of their experiences and choices.

This article explores elements of a successful ministry to women who have experienced generational poverty. This approach is grounded in the belief that genuine Christian compassion coupled with practical support can break the chains of generational poverty. This model also recognizes that the greatest resource a ministry can provide is the transformational power of the Gospel, a personal relationship with Jesus Christ.

Building Trust

Building trust with women who have experienced generational poverty is a multifaceted process that requires empathy, understanding, and a genuine commitment to their well-being. Women within these communities may face various social, economic, and emotional barriers that impact their ability to trust others and engage in supportive relationships. To effectively build trust with these women, it is crucial to adopt a holistic approach that addresses their unique needs and circumstances.

First and foremost, empathy serves as the cornerstone of trust-building. Understanding the lived experiences and challenges of women who have endured generational poverty is essential for establishing meaningful connections. Rather than approaching them with preconceived judgments or stereotypes, it is vital to listen attentively to their stories, validate their feelings, and demonstrate genuine compassion. Empathetic engagement fosters a sense of recognition, signaling to these women that their experiences are respected.

Additionally, trust-building requires a recognition of power dynamics and a commitment to fostering autonomy. Women in poverty often navigate systems they deem inequitable which can erode trust in institutions and individuals. As such, it is crucial to empower these women by involving them in decision-making processes and respecting their right to self-determination. By prioritizing collaboration and partnership, rather than paternalism or top-down approaches, trust can be nurtured within these relationships.

Furthermore, trust-building efforts must be rooted in consistency, reliability, and transparency. Many women who have experienced generational poverty have encountered broken promises, unreliable support systems, and other barriers that exacerbate feelings of mistrust. Therefore, it is essential to demonstrate reliability by following through on commitments, maintaining open lines of communication, and being transparent about intentions and limitations. Consistent and dependable support helps to establish a sense of security and predictability, which are essential for fostering trust over time.

Cultural competence and humility are also indispensable components of trust-building with women from impoverished backgrounds. Recognizing the combination of their identities and the unique cultural factors that shape their experiences is crucial for establishing authentic connections. It is essential to approach these relationships with humility, acknowledging that one's own perspectives and experiences may differ significantly from those of the women being served. By prioritizing cultural humility and actively seeking to understand diverse worldviews, trust can be built on a foundation of mutual respect and appreciation for differences.

Moreover, trust-building efforts should be accompanied by tangible support and resources that meet their everyday needs. Survival is often the dominate concern for women experiencing generational poverty. They witnessed that mindset in their own mothers and grandmothers. Often that concern is directed toward providing for their children. Trust is reinforced through actions that demonstrate a genuine commitment to meeting basic needs and improving their quality of life.

Building trust with women who have experienced generational poverty requires a comprehensive and compassionate approach that addresses their unique needs, challenges, and lived experiences. By fostering empathy, independence, demonstrating reliability, practicing cultural humility, and providing tangible support, meaningful connections can be forged based on trust, respect, and mutual understanding.

Focusing On Strengths and Potential

Empowering women who have experienced generational poverty to understand their strengths, recognize their potential, and set meaningful goals is essential for breaking the cycle of poverty and fostering long-term self-sufficiency. Generational poverty often creates a pervasive sense of hopelessness and self-doubt, as women may internalize negative stereotypes that limit their opportunities for personal and professional growth. Helping these women to cultivate a positive self-image, identify their inherent strengths, and envision a brighter future is foundational to their journey towards empowerment and economic independence.

First, it is crucial to foster a strengths-based approach that acknowledges and celebrates their unique talents and skills. Rather than focusing solely on deficits or challenges, empowering interventions should highlight women's inherent strengths, such as perseverance, resourcefulness, creativity, and compassion. By reframing their narratives and emphasizing their capabilities, women are better equipped to recognize their worth and potential, laying the groundwork for setting meaningful goals and pursuing pathways to success.

Self-awareness and reflection serve as fundamental tools for women to understand their strengths and values and align them with their personal and professional aspirations. Providing opportunities for self-assessment, goal-setting exercises, and life skills workshops can help women explore their interests and envision the kind of future they desire for themselves and their families. Encouraging reflection on past achievements, challenges overcome, and lessons learned can also bolster self-confidence and resilience, empowering women to face life with greater determination and optimism.

Moreover, goal setting is a powerful tool for empowering women to translate their aspirations into actionable steps and measurable outcomes. Setting realistic, achievable goals that are aligned with their values, strengths, and long-term vision is essential for building momentum and sustaining motivation. Encouraging women to break down larger goals into smaller, manageable tasks, and celebrating incremental progress along the way helps to reinforce a sense of accomplishment. Additionally, providing support and accountability mechanisms, such as mentorship, coaching, or peer support groups, can help women stay focused, overcome setbacks, and stay on track toward achieving their goals.

Incorporating a trauma-informed approach is also critical when supporting women who have experienced generational poverty, as many may have endured adverse childhood experiences that impacted their self-esteem and mental well-being. Creating safe, supportive environments is essential to facilitate healing. Offering trauma-informed counseling, support groups, and holistic wellness services can help women address past traumas, build resilience, and cultivate a positive sense of self-worth as they embark on their journey towards empowerment.

Recognizing that the goals and aspirations of women in poverty are diverse and multifaceted is also essential. Programs should emphasize not only economic independence but also personal growth, family well-being, and community engagement. Empowering women to set goals that encompass various domains of their lives, such as education, career advancement, financial stability, health and wellness, and social connections, ensures a holistic approach to empowerment that addresses their complex needs and aspirations.

Helping women who have experienced generational poverty to understand their strengths, recognize their potential, and set meaningful goals is a transformative process that requires empathy, support, and a strengths-based approach. By fostering self-awareness and agency, and by providing resources, tools, and support systems, women can break free from cycles of poverty, and realize their full potential.

Providing Education And Skills Development

Helping women who have experienced generational poverty develop job and life skills while continuing their education is crucial for breaking the cycle of poverty and empowering them to build brighter futures for themselves and their families. Generational poverty often creates significant barriers to accessing education and employment opportunities, perpetuating a cycle of economic hardship and limited mobility. By providing targeted support, resources, and opportunities for educational and skill development, these women can be equipped with the tools and confidence they need to succeed in the workforce and beyond.

One key strategy for helping women develop job and life skills is through the provision of comprehensive education and training programs tailored to their needs and aspirations. These programs should offer a diverse range of learning opportunities, including adult education, vocational training, job readiness workshops, and life skills development. By incorporating hands-on learning experiences, real-world applications, and mentorship opportunities, women can gain practical skills and knowledge that are directly applicable to their career goals and daily lives.

Additionally, fostering a supportive, collaborative learning environment promotes engagement and retention among these women. Creating safe spaces where they feel empowered to take educational risks and learn from their mistakes fosters a sense of belonging and self-confidence, laying the foundation for lifelong learning and personal growth.

Furthermore, providing financial assistance, scholarships, transportation vouchers, and on-site childcare services can help mitigate barriers they may have experienced in the past. The opportunity to learn can inspire them to learn and facilitate greater participation and success in education and training programs.

Moreover, integrating technology into education and training initiatives can enhance accessibility, flexibility, and relevance for women in poverty, many of whom may face digital literacy barriers. Offering online courses, virtual mentorship opportunities, and digital skills training can help women build confidence and proficiency in using technology for learning, communication, and career advancement.

In addition to job-specific skills, it is essential to provide women with holistic life skills that empower them to navigate various aspects of their lives successfully. These may include financial literacy, time management, communication skills, conflict resolution, stress management, and self-care practices. By equipping women with these essential life skills, they can make better decisions, manage their resources effectively, and cultivate healthy relationships and well-being.

Moreover, creating pathways for women to continue their education beyond traditional academic settings, such as adult education programs, community colleges, online courses, and apprenticeship opportunities, enables them to pursue higher levels of education and training that align with their career goals and interests. By promoting lifelong learning and skill development, women can adapt to changing economic trends, seize new opportunities, and achieve long-term economic stability and self-sufficiency.

Assisting women who have experienced generational poverty develop job and life skills while continuing their education is a transformative investment that unlocks doors to economic opportunity, social mobility, and personal fulfillment. By providing targeted support, resources, and opportunities for skill development and education, we can empower women to overcome barriers, realize their full potential, and build brighter futures for themselves, their families, and their communities.

Offering Mentor Relationships

Developing a peer mentor program for women who have experienced generational poverty is a powerful strategy for fostering support and movement toward accomplishing goals. Peer mentorship leverages the lived experiences, wisdom, and mutual understanding among women from similar backgrounds to provide guidance, encouragement, and practical assistance in navigating the challenges of poverty and pursuing pathways to success. By establishing a structured and supportive mentorship framework, women to learn from one another, build meaningful relationships, and access resources and support systems that promote their personal and professional growth.

The first step in developing a peer mentor program is to identify and recruit mentors who have firsthand experience with generational poverty and are willing to share their knowledge, skills, and insights with others. Mentors should possess effective communication skills, empathy, resilience, and a commitment to supporting the empowerment and well-being of their peers. It is essential to provide mentors with comprehensive training and ongoing support to ensure they are equipped to effectively help others, set boundaries, and address potential challenges that may arise during the mentoring process.

Once mentors have been recruited and trained, the next step is to match them with women based on shared interests, goals, and needs. Building rapport and trust between mentors and mentees is crucial for establishing a supportive and productive mentoring relationship. Mentors should take the time to get to know their mentees, listen attentively to their experiences and aspirations, and provide personalized guidance and encouragement tailored to their unique circumstances.

To facilitate meaningful interactions and engagement, it is essential to establish clear goals, expectations, and guidelines for the mentorship program. This may include defining the scope of the mentoring relationship, establishing regular meeting schedules, and outlining topics or activities for discussion and exploration. Providing mentorship resources, tools, and templates can also help mentors and mentees navigate their roles effectively and maximize the impact of their interactions.

In addition to one-on-one mentoring relationships, incorporating group activities, workshops, and networking opportunities into the peer mentor program can foster a sense of community, belonging, and mutual support among participants. Group activities provide opportunities for the women to connect with one another, share their experiences, learn from collective wisdom, and build social connections and networks of support. Moreover, workshops and skill-building sessions can enhance participants' knowledge, confidence, and capacity to navigate various aspects of their lives successfully.

Regular monitoring, evaluation, and feedback mechanisms are essential for assessing the effectiveness of the peer mentor program and identifying areas for improvement. Collecting feedback from mentors, mentees, and program stakeholders allows for ongoing reflection, learning, and adaptation to ensure the program meets the evolving needs and aspirations of participants. Moreover, celebrating successes, acknowledging achievements, and recognizing the contributions of mentors and mentees helps to reinforce a culture of support, gratitude, and empowerment within the program.

Developing a peer mentor program for women who have experienced generational poverty is a transformative approach to fostering support, empowerment, and resilience. By utilizing the power of peer relationships and lived experiences, women can learn from one another, build meaningful connections, and access resources and support systems that promote growth. Through structured mentorship relationships, group activities, and ongoing evaluation and feedback, the women can overcome barriers, realize their full potential, and build brighter futures for themselves, their families.

Providing Spiritual Support

Developing a spiritual support program for women who have experienced generational poverty can provide a powerful framework from which they can build lives filled with a sense of worth, strength, and hope. Spirituality can be broadly defined as a sense of connection to something greater than oneself. It can encompass beliefs, values, and practices that provide meaning, purpose, and strength in the face of adversity. For the purposes of this article, spirituality is defined as having a personal relationship with God through Jesus Christ.

The first step in developing a spiritual support program is to create a safe and inclusive space where women feel comfortable exploring and expressing their spiritual beliefs, experiences, and aspirations. This may involve establishing a welcoming environment free from judgment where women from diverse religious and cultural backgrounds feel valued, respected, and supported in their spiritual journeys.

Once the foundation for a supportive community has been established, the next step is to offer a range of spiritual resources, practices, and activities that promote the development of a relationship with God. These may include prayer, Bible studies, journaling, worship experiences, and reflective discussions on spiritual matters. The goal is for the women to solidify their relationship with God which provides them with the most powerful resource they could ever have to move forward with their lives. Providing that support can help women cultivate a deeper sense of meaning and purpose for their lives. Understanding that God has a plan for their lives provides direction and motivation.

Offering a spiritual support program that includes local church attendance provides women in need with additional benefits.

Opportunities to connect with other believers fosters continued spiritual growth. Being a part of a faith community also provides the added support these women need to succeed.

Developing a spiritual support program for women who have experienced generational poverty can provide them with the most powerful resource of all, a life-changing relationship with God. That relationship helps them know that they are never alone.

Celebrating Progress and Achievement

Celebrating progress in a program for women who have experienced generational poverty is vital to the development of a positive self-image. Acknowledging and celebrating milestones, no matter how small, promotes confidence toward making even greater achievements. Consider the following suggestions.

Celebrate all individual achievements, whether it is completing a training course, securing employment, achieving a personal goal, or overcoming a challenge. Acknowledge the efforts and perseverance of each participant, highlighting their strengths and contributions to their own progress.

Tailor celebrations to the preferences and interests of individual participants, ensuring that they feel valued and seen. This might include personalized certificates or tokens of appreciation that reflect the unique journey and accomplishments of each woman.

Community Celebrations: Organize positive community-wide celebrations that bring participants, mentors, program staff, and stakeholders together to commemorate collective progress and success. These events can include award ceremonies, cultural performances, storytelling sessions, or banquets, fostering a sense of belonging and solidarity among participants.

Provide opportunities for participants to share their success stories and lessons learned with one another and the broader community. This not only inspires others but also reinforces the narrative of possibility and resilience within the program, demonstrating that positive change is achievable.

Encourage participants to provide feedback on the program and its impact, empowering them to shape and improve future initiatives. Actively listen to their suggestions, concerns, and ideas for how to enhance the program and make it more responsive to their needs and aspirations.

Beyond immediate celebrations, consider ways to provide ongoing recognition and support for participants as they continue on their journeys toward self-sufficiency. This might include alumni networks, mentorship opportunities, or leadership development programs that enable participants to pay it forward and support others in their communities.

Celebrating progress in a program for women who have experienced generational poverty is about more than just marking milestones. By recognizing achievements, sharing success stories, and empowering participants to shape the program's future, the women understand that their achievements are worthy of recognition and celebration; that they are becoming the person they have always dreamed of being. That is the power of celebrating progress.

Offering Long-Term Support

Providing long-term support for women who have experienced generational poverty is essential for breaking the cycle of poverty, fostering resilience, and promoting sustainable pathways to self-sufficiency. Generational poverty often creates complex and interrelated challenges that require ongoing assistance, guidance, and resources.

One key component of long-term support is access to education and skill-building opportunities that empower women to pursue their academic and career goals. This may include scholarships, grants, and financial assistance for higher education or vocational training programs, as well as ongoing mentorship, coaching, and academic support services to help women navigate their educational journeys successfully. By investing in their continued learning and professional development, we can equip women with the knowledge, skills, and confidence they need to access meaningful employment opportunities and achieve long-term economic stability.

Moreover, providing access to affordable housing, childcare, and other essential services is crucial for addressing the basic needs and well-being of women and their families. By partnering with community organizations and social service agencies, the women can access resources and support systems that promote their physical, emotional, and mental well-being. This may include case management, counseling, access to healthcare services, and assistance with navigating social welfare programs and entitlements.

Building supportive relationships and social connections is another important aspect of long-term support for women who have experienced generational poverty. By fostering a sense of belonging and community, women can access peer support, mentorship, and friendship networks that provide encouragement and, accountability. This may involve organizing support groups, peer mentorship programs, or community events that bring women together to share their experiences, celebrate their achievements, and support one another through life's challenges.

Furthermore, offering ongoing support for personal and professional development, including financial literacy, life skills training, and career advancement services, helps women build resilience and adaptability in the face of changing circumstances. By equipping women with the tools and resources they need to navigate life's challenges and seize opportunities for growth and self-improvement, we can empower them to realize their full potential and achieve their goals.

Providing long-term support for women who have experienced generational poverty requires a comprehensive and holistic approach that addresses their multifaceted needs and aspirations. By investing in education and skill-building opportunities, access to essential services, supportive relationships and social connections, along with ongoing personal and professional development, we can empower women to break free from cycles of poverty, overcome barriers, and build brighter futures for themselves and their families.

Conclusion

Addressing the multifaceted needs of women experiencing generational poverty requires a comprehensive and holistic ministry program. Through initiatives focused on building trust, recognizing strengths and potential, providing education and skill development, offering mentorship opportunities, providing spiritual support, celebrating achievement, and offering long-term assistance, transformative pathways can be created which lead to self-sufficiency and success.

By embracing these principles and providing these opportunities women can realize that they are made in the image of God which ascribes to them dignity, worth, and potential regardless of their socioeconomic background. Once they discover who they are in Christ and receive needed training and support, these women can fulfill God's plan and purposes for their lives and their families and serve as examples for other women with similar struggles. Please consider how God might use you to develop a support ministry for women facing generational poverty.

MINISTRY INVENTORY GUIDE: ASSESS YOUR CHURCH'S MINISTRY CAPACITY AND IDENTITY

By Heidi Unruh
Congregations, Community Outreach and
Leadership Development Project
unruhheidi@aol.com

Revised 2009

*The Ministry Inventory Guide was created originally for the CD-ROM
workbook "Becoming a Church That Makes a Difference," created in
partnership with the Word & Deed Network
of Evangelicals for Social Action
(www.urbanministry.org/esa/wordanddeed).
This Guide was developed with support from Compassion Coalition,
Knoxville, TN (www.compassioncoalition.org).*

MINISTRY INVENTORY GUIDE

Overview

The Ministry Inventory consists of ten areas of questions related to the congregation's outreach (including all forms of evangelism and service). The questions focus on local outreach, but do not exclude international missions. Some questions ask about *what* the church does, others focus on *how* and *why* the church engages in external ministry.

1. Ministry History
2. Ministry Activities
3. Ministry Organization
4. Ministry Assets
5. Ministry Connections and Collaborations
6. Ministry Balance
7. Ministry Involvement: Evangelism
8. Ministry Involvement: Social Action
9. Ministry Bridges and Barriers
10. Ministry Outcomes

Note that at the bottom of each page of the inventory guide are "summary reflection" questions, which invite real-time comments by participants on what they have learned through the discussion.

The ministry inventory takes stock of the overall status of ministry at your church. You may opt to follow up with a more in-depth program evaluation for each major outreach program (see the *Program Revision and Evaluation Guide* on www.fastennetwork.org).

1. Ministry History

Each church's external mission reflects its unique history and heritage. Looking at where the church has been, can be helpful in planning its next steps.

a) *Ministry heritage:* Is there anything in the story of the founding of your church that relates to mission and local outreach? What do you know about a missional heritage in your denomination (if your church belongs to one)?

b) *Ministry history:* When has your church been at its best in missional outreach? Has the congregation ever gotten "burned"? Have there been conflicts surrounding outreach, and how have they been resolved? Create a timeline of major church efforts relating to evangelism, social action, or global mission over the church's history, including discontinued ministries, key partnerships, major changes in ministry funding or leadership, and new initiatives planned for the future. How does this history of ministry engagement correspond with high and low points in the overall life of your church?

c) *Main characters:* Who has played a key role in the church's ministry development? Tell about "heroes/heroines" or "saints" in the church who have made a difference in the community or beyond.

d) *Ministry record:* Which ministry efforts do members point to with pride, and which have not worked out so well? What has generated the most excitement, and what has been like pulling teeth? Complete this sentence: "The most successful ministry we have undertaken is ..." What factors made this a positive ministry experience?

e) *Ministry identity:* Which of the following images best describes the character of your church's ministry over its history:
  - *Pillar* churches are a stable civic anchor in the community.
  - *Pilgrim* churches provide a shelter for minority groups and immigrant cultures.
  - *Survivor* churches take risks to stand with people on the social margins.
  - *Prophet* churches proactively challenge immorality and injustice in the world.
  - *Servant* churches quietly provide help to individuals in

need, near and far.

- *Family* churches support their members as a close-knit, caring group.
- *Lighthouse* churches seek to shine the gospel to those who are unchurched.
- *Entrepreneur* churches are catalysts for community development.
- *Yeast* churches exercise influence primarily through individual members.
- *Other*-- come up with your own image.

See Carl S. Dudley and Sally A. Johnson, *Energizing the*

Congregation: Images that Shape Your Congregation's Ministry (Louisville, KY: Westminster/Knox, 1993).

Summary reflections:

- What main themes emerged in the responses to these questions?
- Did you gain a helpful perspective on your church's outreach, learn anything surprising about your church, or spark ideas for ministry through this exercise?

2. Ministry Activities

As your church considers how to expand or enhance its outreach, a good place to start is by developing an accurate portrait of the church's current involvement.

a) *Ministry focus:* Has the church identified one or more particular ministry communities — the neighborhood around the church, another geographic location, or a specific population (e.g., college students, immigrants, people with disabilities)? What are the main social and spiritual needs represented in this community?

b) *Ministry programs:* Use the "Directory of External Ministry Programs" worksheet to record an overview of current programs designed to serve spiritual or social needs beyond the congregation. For each major outreach program (if there are many programs, select the five that are

most significant to the church), additionally provide a
short profile, including:

- a description of what the program does, noting
  how the ministry addresses spiritual and / or social needs;
- the audience or area that the ministry serves;
- the intended goals and actual outcomes (if
  known) of the program;
- how the ministry draws on, partners with, or
  strengthens assets in the community (e.g., recruiting parents as volunteers in a children's ministry,
  partnering with the local business council for a
  job training program)
- a brief history of the program;
- (if possible) a story illustrating the need for this
  ministry, or a "success" case.

c) *Benevolence:* Over the past three years, what kinds of people have been asking the church for aid, and what have
   been their needs? How do they find out about your
   church as a place that can offer help? How has the church
   responded to them? Does the church have policies to
   guide its charitable assistance? What challenges / problems / opportunities have been associated with benevolence?

d) *Informal outreach:* How does the church encourage members to witness to and serve others in their daily lives,
   and to what extent does this happen? How does the
   church facilitate opportunities for people in the congregation to form relationships with people who are not Christians or who are on the social margins?

e) *Member ministry:* How are individual members or small
   groups involved by their own initiative in addressing
   particular social concerns, or ministering in an unofficial
   way? (For example, a member who consistently speaks
   out on behalf of pro-life issues, a family that takes an annual mission trip to Mexico, a cluster of members who
   volunteer regularly for Habitat for Humanity, or a small

group that pushes the church to be more environmentally friendly)

Summary reflections:

- What main themes emerged in the responses to these questions?
- Did you gain a helpful perspective on your church's outreach, learn anything surprising about your church, or spark ideas for ministry through this exercise?

3. Ministry Organization

Carl Dudley notes in *Community Ministry*, "In our common concern for social ministry, the way we mobilize in each congregation is unique to the people involved and the problems they face." When it comes to outreach, how does your church get things done?

a) *Decision-making*: What is the process for making and implementing decisions that involve the church's outreach (for example, launching a new ministry, allocating funding, assigning leadership)? What values or principles guide these decisions? What kinds of informal, "behind the scenes" activity goes into decision-making?

b) *Planning*: Does the church have a strategic plan for ministry development, or does it develop more spontaneously? Is there a central focus or set of priorities that guides outreach, and/or are efforts scattered in various unrelated directions? Does the church have a vision statement for its community ministry?

c) *Organizational structure:* How is external mission reflected in the organizational structure of the church? Is there a place for outreach goals in staff job descriptions, the committee structure, the budget format, etc.?

d) *Volunteer management and support:* What is the church's system for recruiting, training, placing, tracking, evaluating, and recognizing volunteers? What opportunities do members have to share with one another about the ministry work they are doing outside the congregation, and ask other members to contribute (i.e., volunteer time, in-kind goods, donations, prayer support)?

e) *Leadership:* Where do ideas, energy and initiative for outreach ministry come from — pastors, lay leaders, small groups, individual members, community leaders? Note which of these tasks represent current leadership strengths and challenges: starting new initiatives, sustaining, and growing programs, mobilizing church members, ministry evaluation and accountability, networking, and partnerships, cultivating resources for ministry, long-range vision

Summary reflections:

- What main themes emerged in the responses to these questions?

Did you gain a helpful perspective on your church's outreach, learn anything surprising about your church, or spark ideas for ministry through this exercise?

4. Ministry Assets

What resources for ministry does your church have to work with? Inventory the major assets — tangible and intangible — available to the congregation, and note the extent to which they are currently being used for external ministry:

a) *Financial resources:* Endowment, tithes, mission offerings, fundraisers, major donors, grants, etc. What is the church's overall financial health? How much of the budget currently goes toward external ministry? (note local vs. international)

b) *Material resources:* Building, equipment, vehicles, educational curricula, etc.

c) *Human resources:*
- List staff and volunteers from the congregation engaged in outreach.

- Identify potential human resources from outside the congregation (e.g., consultants, interns, community volunteers).
- Note special skills and interests that are represented in your congregation (managerial, electrical, artistic, health care, cooking, etc.).

d) *Intangible resources:* Intangible assets (which are often overlooked) include:

- Reputation: A positive reputation in the community, a proven ministry track record, or association with a trusted community service organization.
- Visibility: Recognition outside the church, gained for example by consistently sending representatives to community meetings.
- Energy: Momentum for ministry flowing from spiritual dynamism, a passion to make a difference, a positive outlook, and youthful (or young at heart) enthusiasm.
- Time: Who in the congregation has time to share with others? Consider the volunteer potential of stay-at-home parents, college students, people with disabilities who do not work, and retirees.
- Trust in leaders: A healthy respect for leaders that encourages the congregation to follow leaders down new paths of faith in action.
- Ministry experiences: Motivational stories of past ministry achievements, or the encouragement of members who have led by example.
- Connections: Access to people or institutions who could contribute to ministry — e.g., donors, banks, colleges, politicians, foundations, artists, hospitals, etc.

e) *Spiritual resources:* What main biblical or theological foundations for outreach mission are taught at your church? What role models or sources of inspiration are important to your understanding of mission (e.g., denominational legacy, Christian authors or speakers, other churches, or church leaders, etc.)?

Summary reflections:

- What main themes emerged in the responses to these

questions?

- Did you gain a helpful perspective on your church's outreach, learn anything surprising about your church, or spark ideas for ministry through this exercise?

5. Ministry Connections and Collaborations

No church is — or should be — a lone ranger when it comes to outreach. Every church is embedded in relationships with the broader community, with the wider Christian fellowship, and with ministry partners. What connections does your church have with other organizations, and how does your church relate to its community?

a) *Partners*: What outside groups does the church connect with to carry out ministry goals (e.g. the denomination, foundations, community agencies, para-church organizations, church coalitions, government, etc.)? What kinds of cooperative arrangements exist between the church and these outside entities (e.g., shared space or equipment, jointly sponsored programs, collaborative fundraising projects)? How healthy are these partnerships?

b) *Community relations*: What community events or programs has the church hosted or participated in? Does the church ever invite local leaders or agencies to special church events? Has the church sought out people from the community to help plan, take part in, or give feedback on church projects that affect the community (such as ministry programs, building projects or outdoor services)?

c) *Associations:* Does the church or pastor participate in local or national associations or networks such as a pastor's prayer group, a community organizing coalition, a denominational association, Christian Community Development Association, etc.?

d) *Representation*: Does the pastor or other church leader represent the church in some official capacity out in the community, such as on a public task force or the board of a non-profit agency?

e) *Guidelines*: What principles (if any) guide the church's selection of partner agencies and projects — for example, whether to participate in secular or ecumenical projects, or whether to accept government funding?

Summary reflections:

- What main themes emerged in the responses to these questions?

- Did you gain a helpful perspective on your church's outreach, learn anything surprising about your church, or spark ideas for ministry through this exercise?

6. Ministry Balance

Maintaining a healthy church is a continual balancing act. Church life involves multiple, competing, dynamics: in-reach and outreach, local and global mission, evangelism, and social compassion. It helps to step back and assess these dynamics with a big-picture perspective.

a) *Nurture/outreach*: What is the balance between ministries of internal congregational nurture, and outreach ministry to those outside the church? Which is your church's priority, in terms of staff and volunteer time, resources, attention from the pulpit, etc.? How satisfied is the congregation with this balance?

b) *Mission focus*: What is the balance between local and global mission? Which is your church's priority, in terms of staff and volunteer time, resources, attention from the pulpit, etc.? How satisfied is the congregation with this balance?

c) *Evangelism/social ministry*: What is the balance between evangelism and social outreach? Which is your church's priority, in terms of staff and volunteer time, resources, attention from the pulpit, etc.? How satisfied is the congregation with this balance?

d) *Integration*: How much overlap or integration is there between evangelism and social activism? Are they totally separate ministries, interconnected ministries, or integrated within the same ministries? Do compassion and evangelism ministries serve the same community, or are they focused on different groups of people?

e) *Top down / bottom up:* What is the balance between ministries that are initiated and organized by church leadership (top down), and ministries that grow more informally out of the interests and involvement of members (bottom up)?

Summary reflections:

- What main themes emerged in the responses to these questions?

- Did you gain a helpful perspective on your church's outreach, learn anything surprising about your church, or spark ideas for ministry through this exercise?

7. Ministry Involvement: Evangelism

The following questions can help you take a closer look at how your congregation is sharing the good news of salvation with others.

a) *Who?* Does the church primarily reach out to people who are already Christians and looking for a new church home, lapsed or "baby" Christians in need of spiritual renewal and discipleship, or people who are not yet Christians? Is there an "ideal" type of person or family whom the church has been seeking to reach?

b) *How?* Is the church's witness to Christ:

- *Explicit* (e.g., sharing testimonies or tracts) and/or *implicit* (e.g., modeled through lifestyle and service)?

- *Formal* (through organized church programs or campaigns) and/or *informal* (through relationships, in the course of members' daily lives)?

- *Event-based* (e.g., reaching groups of people via revival services or concerts) and/or *one-on-one* (e.g., sharing with one person at a time, such as in door-to-door evangelism)?

Why does the church have this approach? What feedback have leaders and members provided about the way the church engages in evangelism?

c) *How much?* How often do evangelistic events or campaigns take place? About what percentage of the congregation is involved in evangelism? What feedback have leaders and members provided about the amount of evangelism that the congregation is doing — too much emphasis, not enough, just right?

d) *Training and recruitment:* What programs of evangelism training are in place? How are people recruited to participate? How strongly does the leadership promote evangelism?

e) *Attitude:* How would you summarize the congregation's attitude toward evangelism — enthusiastic, eager but anxious, terrified, resistant, apathetic?

Summary reflections:

- What main themes emerged in the responses to these questions?

- Did you gain a helpful perspective on your church's outreach, learn anything surprising about your church, or spark ideas for ministry through this exercise?

8. Ministry Involvement: Social Action

The following questions can help you take a closer look at how your congregation is demonstrating God's love through ministries of compassion and justice.

a) *How?* Which of these areas of social action does the church emphasize:

- Meeting immediate needs by providing goods and services (relief);

- Supporting people by teaching skills or character, or offering emotional support (personal empowerment);

- Renewing the economic and institutional building blocks of a healthy community (community development); and/or

- Reforming political, economic, or cultural systems (systemic change).

Why does the church have this approach? What feedback have leaders and members provided about the way the church engages in social ministry

b) *How much?* About what percentage of the congregation is involved in social ministry? What feedback have leaders and members provided about the amount of social ministry that the congregation is doing — too much emphasis, not enough, just right?

c) *Training and recruitment:* How are members recruited and equipped to participate in social ministries? How strongly does the leadership promote social ministry?

d) *Attitude:* How would you summarize the congregation's attitude toward social action—enthusiastic, eager but anxious, cynical, terrified, resistant, apathetic?

e) *Holistic approach:* Does the church seek to address the spiritual needs of the people served in social ministries (e.g., by offering prayer and sharing the gospel in non-coercive ways)? Are people served by social ministries welcomed into the church? (Does the church nurture the spiritual development of ministry staff and volunteers, and help them connect their ministry involvement with their faith?

Summary reflections:

- What main themes emerged in the responses to these questions?
- Did you gain a helpful perspective on your church's outreach, learn anything surprising about your church, or spark ideas for ministry through this exercise?

9. Ministry Bridges and Barriers

Transformational community ministry entails building bridges — both to welcome the community into the church, and to bring the church out into the community. Consider possible sources of barriers to relationship with those whom God has called your congregation to love in Christ's name.

a) *Reputation*: What is your church known for in the surrounding community? How do you think someone who does not attend might describe your congregation? Are you viewed as being *for* the community, or simply *in* the community?

b) *Preconceptions*: Do people in the congregation have prejudices, stereotypes, or a history of negative interactions with people in the community that might be a barrier to authentic, caring relationships? Does the congregation tend to fear the community or think of it as a "bad neighborhood"?

c) *Inclusivity:* How welcoming is your congregation of people who are different — in terms of economic class, race, language, appearance, physical or mental abilities, and family structure? Are members gracious toward newcomers who behave or dress in unconventional ways? How does your church help people who are spiritual seekers or new Christians feel at home, socially and spiritually?

d) *Geography:* Where do members live in relationship to the church — are they mostly commuters, or community residents? What kinds of natural connections exist between the church and community, such as members who live, work, own businesses or go to school there? Does the church provide opportunities for members to get to know the church's neighbors?

e) *Facilities:* Are there physical barriers that represent symbolic obstacles to newcomers (e.g., fences, walls, "no trespassing" signs, locked gates, lack of handicap accessibility)? Do the church grounds say to people, "We care about the appearance of this neighborhood and we care about you"?

f) *Priorities*: How visible is the congregation's investment in the well-being of its neighbors? To what extent is a commitment to community outreach incorporated into "routine" aspects of church life?

- Is the importance of outreach in word and deed affirmed in the mission statement, membership covenant, welcome brochure, website, etc?

- Are the needs and dreams of the community present in congregational prayers, church bulletin boards, newsletters, etc.?

- Is Christian responsibility beyond the walls of the church addressed in sermons, Sunday school classes, small group Bible studies, literature in the church library or bookstore, etc.?

Summary reflections:

- What main themes emerged in the responses to these questions?

- Did you gain a helpful perspective on your church's outreach, learn anything surprising about your church, or spark ideas for ministry through this exercise?

10. Ministry Outcomes

Holistic ministry means planting seeds of faith. Expect a harvest! (Galatians 6:9) What fruit have you seen from your kingdom work? Keep in mind that the ultimate test of ministry is faithfulness to God's calling. (See also the *Ministry Program Evaluation and Revision Guide on* www.fastennetwork.org for a more detailed assessment of individual programs.)

a) What have been the observable outcomes of the church's outreach (whether focused on evangelism and/or and social action), on two levels:

- *quantitative* — record of ministry goals achieved or numbers of people who share in the desired ministry benefits (advocacy goals met; conversions, rededications, or new members; GED program graduates; families in new housing; etc.). How are these numbers tracked, if at all?

- *qualitative* — description of general positive outcomes (improvements in the overall quality of life in the community, transformation in individual lives)

(Keep in mind that *more* ministry does not always

mean *better quality* ministry!)

b) Is it important to your church to evaluate its external ministries, and if so, how are outcomes evaluated? What feedback have leaders, members and beneficiaries provided about the outcomes of the church's outreach ministries? Does the church have a sense that its ministries are "working" or not, and why this is so?

c) Which specific ministries (current and past) have been considered the most effective? What was successful about it? What factors led to the good results?

d) What have been the outcomes of outreach ministry for the church itself, both positive and negative, in the following areas:
   - discipleship and spiritual vitality
   - member involvement with and commitment to the church
   - leadership development
   - church size and resource levels
   - conflict

   If the church's outreach has had minimal impact on the congregation, explore why.

e) Does the church have a long-range vision or broad goals for its community outreach? How will the church know if it is on track with these goals – what are the benchmarks or signs of progress?

Summary reflections:

- What main themes emerged in the responses to these questions?

- Did you gain a helpful perspective on your church's outreach, learn anything surprising about your church, or spark ideas for ministry through this exercise?

INTERPRETING THE MINISTRY INVENTORY

Use the following reflection questions to guide the interpretation of the information you gathered in the ministry inventory. As a team, set aside time for discussing these questions in an atmosphere of worshipful reflection. Engage the leadership of the church in this process as appropriate.

The reflection questions help you to take stock of what your church brings to the goal of loving your community in Christ's name, as well as where it may need to grow. Each of these questions has two parts: *assess* and *act*. Drawing on the reports and worksheets, first *assess* where your church is in its missional journey, and then decide how to *act* on this information.

This process is important preparation for the next steps of enhancing the impact of existing outreach and planning new ministry opportunities.

Ministry Inventory Reflection Questions

1. *What are your church's passions and dreams for community ministry?*

What we are passionate about -- what we do with the most energy and joy -- inevitably shapes our agenda. Tap into your church's current "hot spots" for ministry.

Assess:

A. Who in the church (individuals or groups) has been most invested in holistic ministry, and why? What are they most passionate about?

B. What issues, causes, activities, or goals have generated the most significant response in the congregation? Based on patterns of involvement, what types of ministries might members be most (and least) likely to support?

Act:

A. Invite those who have been quiet champions of kingdom ministry to share their stories with the congregation. Their energy can be contagious!

B. Write out a set of goals or dreams for change (for both church and community) that captures the current values and vision of the congregation.

2. *What are your church's strengths and assets for holistic ministry?*

Celebrate what your church is already doing well and take inventory of your capacity for future ministry.

Assess:

A. Consider this quote: "A congregation is more likely to move into a new area of ministry if they can see it as reasserting or claiming something good that they have always been than if they are asked to change into something new and different" (Phil Tom and Sally Johnson, *Handbook for Urban Church Ministries*, p. 20). Where do you find the "good that you have always been" in your history, identity, or current activities? What have you done, or could you do, with excellence?

B. Take stock of your untapped potential. Develop a list of strengths that the church can draw on for local mission. Assets can be tangible (e.g., property, funds, people) or intangible (e.g., skill sets, reputation, experience, connections).

Most congregational characteristics could become ministry assets. For example, a large building opens up space for ministry programs. Having a close-knit congregation that cares for one another could be an asset for a mentoring ministry that adopts a struggling family. A reputation for great children's ministries provides a natural bridge for outreach to at-risk youth in the community.

Act:

A. Brainstorm ways of capitalizing on these strengths. Use the "Church Outreach Opportunities Worksheet" to help connect ministry assets and interests with simple ways to serve the community and share good news.

B. Share these insights with the congregation. Consider a special worship service to celebrate your church's unique heritage and potential for kingdom service.

3. What are weaknesses and obstacles to holistic ministry?

What hinders the church from developing its capacity for holistic ministry? Obstacles to outreach may include the church's theology, relationship with the community, culture, or past experiences.

The ministry inventory can also help anticipate potential sources of resistance to new ministry initiatives. Change doesn't come easy to any group of people, so expect that taking steps in a new direction may provoke some tensions and conflicts. It may be impossible to avoid resistance altogether, but it helps to be prepared in advance.

Assess:

A. What aspects of holistic ministry are underdeveloped – what could the church do more, or do better? Are there areas in which God may be leading the church to repent for not having fully followed Jesus' example and mandate for kingdom ministry?

B. What are the main roadblocks to more fully embracing an external ministry paradigm and putting it into action? Identify potential sources of friction related to local mission - both internal (e.g., lack of trained ministry leaders, concerns about insurance or damage to church property, history of being "burned" by involvement with people in need), and external (e.g., the community does not see the church as a partner, language/cultural barriers to outreach).

Act:

A. Investigate case studies of other churches or nonprofits that have overcome similar obstacles. If possible, bring a small group of church members to visit a good model, or invite a leader from this group to speak at your church.

B. Consider ways to build momentum for change in the church's outreach and to diminish resistance. Who in the church or community might be recruited as an ally in supporting a new direction for ministry?

4. *What is your church's readiness for holistic ministry?*

   Assess:

A. How healthy is your church? Holistic ministry rests on a foundation of healthy spiritual vitality, relationships, organizational dynamics, and leadership. Are there areas of internal church life that need to be strengthened in order for the congregation to embrace an outward focus?

B. How mission-centered is your church? Does your church have the M&M syndrome — "More and More for Me and Mine"? Or is it turned right-side-up to emphasize a "W-W" gospel — "We are for the World"? How open is the church to a growing commitment to outreach?

   Act:

A. As a pastor remarked: "God makes us whole, and God makes us instruments to bring wholeness to our community." How is God leading the congregation toward greater wholeness? What might be done to cultivate spiritual maturity? To nurture caring, accountable relationships? To develop skills in transformational leadership? To build positive habits of communication and conflict resolution?

B. How could the church be encouraged to share God's heart for a lost and broken world? Create opportunities for teaching and experiences to help members open their eyes to the needs that grieve God's heart, and to taste God's joy when people are redeemed and restored (Luke 15:10).

5. *What are the next steps for your church in its ministry journey?*

Assess:

Given the findings of the ministry inventory, which two or three of the following areas are top priorities for your church's growth toward holistic ministry?

➢ Laying a foundation

☐ *Spiritual foundation:* help the congregation deepen their grasp of the biblical calling to faith in action and renew their spiritual commitment

☐ *Expand awareness:* enlarge the congregation's understanding of community needs, the principles of transformational development, and stories of effective ministry models

☐ *External orientation:* embrace a commitment to outreach mission as part of the church's DNA, integral to the church's organizational structure

☐ *Community connections:* research needs and assets in the community, while networking and building bridges of caring and solidarity with the church's neighbors

☐ *Ministry leadership team:* recruit and equip a core group of emerging leaders to guide the church's ministry journey

➢ Building on the vision

☐ *Seed ministry:* motivate the congregation through first-step service projects or mission trips that expose people to needs and to the experience of serving others

☐ *Ministry vision:* discern practical ministry goals grounded in the desires of community stakeholders, the church's capacity, and the Spirit's leading

☐ *Program development:* organize plans and resources for new outreach programs; expand knowledge and skills related to effective ministry strategies, activities, and administration

☐ *Volunteer mobilization:* equip and energize the congregation to participate in the ministry vision

☐ *Ministry partnerships:* identify and build relationships with individuals, institutions, and other churches with common kingdom goals

➤ Strengthening and sustaining the work

☐ *Evaluation*: Assess current ministry programs to see how they can be more faithful and effective

☐ *Transformational impact:* reorient current ministries to move beyond giving aid to nurture relationships with people in need; beyond individual needs to community-wide dimensions of social problems; and beyond "band-aid" relief to long-term development

☐ *Spiritual nurture:* take steps to enrich the spiritual life of outreach staff and volunteers, and to provide spiritual care for those served by compassion ministries

☐ *Best-practice mentoring:* Seek to learn from other churches more experienced in holistic, transformational ministry

❒ *Renew and refresh:* Take time to express appreciation, celebrate God's work, invest in relationships, reflect on ministry experiences, and recast the vision

Act:

A. For each growth priority identified above, what is a realistic goal or action step that is doable in the next three months? Organize a team plan to carry this out.

> Examples of action steps:
> o *Teach a Sunday school series on biblical compassion*
> o *Invite children in a neighboring housing project to attend the church's annual Vacation Bible School*
> o *Offer the church's building to host neighborhood association meetings*
> o *Host a dialogue with business leaders in the community interested in economic development*
> o *Research grants to support an affordable housing initiative*
> o *Find outreach-oriented curriculum for small groups*
> o *Plan a congregational Habitat for Humanity workday*
> o *Launch a community ministry prayer team*
> o *Host a neighborhood block party*
> o *Create a bulletin board for community events and volunteer/giving opportunities*
> o *Provide budget support for a church member starting up an ESL program*
> o *Form a study group to learn more about the community and explore a shared vision for ministry*

B. What resources or contacts can help you take the steps you have identified? See the ministry resources available on these websites:

o Collaborative for Neighborhood Transformation (www.neighborhoodtransfor-
  mation.net)
o Communities First Association (www.commu-
  nitiesfirstassociation.org)
o ESA Ministry Center (www.esa-online.org)
o Externally Focused Network (www.external-
  lyfocusednetwork.org)
o Faith in Action (www.putyourfaithinac-
  tion.org)
o FASTEN (www.fastennetwork.org)

COMMUNITY STUDY:
A GUIDE TO UNDERSTANDING
YOUR CHURCH'S CONTEXT FOR MINISTRY
by Heidi Unruh

Community analysis enables you to choose a ministry that is really needed, take best advantage of existing community resources, and convince your congregation and other friends that your program is worth supporting. In order to do that, you need to create as thorough and as balanced a profile of your community as you can. . . . God is already at work in your community. Your task is to find out where you can enter the picture. (Handbook for Urban Church Ministries, *p. 13)*

INTRODUCTION: WHY AND HOW TO STUDY YOUR COMMUNITY

Why Study Your Community?

According to Ray Bakke, "Evangelicalism has had a theology of persons and programs, but it lacked a conscious theology of place." To develop effective community ministry, churches must learn to do "exegesis of environments." You must become a student of a neighborhood in order to become its servant.

A community assessment has seven main goals:

1. *To guide strategic planning and the development of new ministries.*

Information improves a church's aim in making prudent, strategic investments with its ministry resources. Without an accurate assessment of the community's needs and strengths, ministry designs may be flawed. Identifying trends also helps the church to be proactive, beyond merely responding to crises.

2. *To help understand the forces that affect the lives of people in the community.*

Individuals are influenced by the demographic, cultural, and institutional forces around them. A community as assessment, reveals (sometimes hidden) dynamics that influence people's opportunities, choices, and perceptions of self-worth.

3. *To help understand community factors that influence ministry effectiveness.*

Ignorance of external influences on its ministries can lead a church to become discouraged, or to fight the wrong battles. Researching community assets allows a church to connect with other resources, to prevent the duplication of services, to identify potential allies, and to take the culture of the community into account.

4. *To draw on stores of motivation and vision in the community.*

For people in the church and community to join together in working toward transformation, they must have a shared vision. A community study process that engages the input of the community, identifying people's passions and potential, can help generate momentum toward organized action.

5. *To build connections between the church and the community.*

A well-drawn portrait of its context can mobilize the church's yearning to see God's "kingdom come" in the community. The process of networking and listening also nourishes the congregation's sense of belonging in the community, and prepares the way for ministry partnerships.

6. *To help understand how the church itself is affected by the community.*

It is important to understand how your church's specific geographic and cultural setting has helped to shape its identity. To remain relevant and viable, churches must be willing to accept and adjust to changing environmental factors.

7. *To discern how your church is perceived by the community.*

Taking the pulse of the community gives you the opportunity to see your church from the community's perspective. Churches are sometimes woefully unaware of, or misled about, their local reputation. "Outsiders'" views of your church can represent a stepping stone—or a barrier—to building effective ministries.

Community Study Process

The community study can be undertaken by a group of 3-4 persons. The best candidates for this group are observant people who appreciate the community and feel that they have a stake in its well-being; who are good networkers and enjoy getting "out and about"; who have a knack at listening to people and pulling together various points of view; and who have time to dedicate to this project.

The first step of a community study is to **define your community of ministry** so that you have identified a distinct geographical area or people group for your community study (and ministry focus). The next step is to gather information about your community, using the variety of methods outlined below. Try to select at least three different methods that fit with your context, so you are getting a well-rounded picture.

After completing the community study, prepare a **report on your findings** to share with the church's leadership. Keep in mind that the goal is a brief overview of the key points, not a doctoral dissertation!

It may be helpful to set a time frame for the community study, so that the research and reporting stages do not continue indefinitely. However, the goal of learning about the community is ongoing. Beyond gathering data, a community study thus entails active **networking** with people and institutions in the community. Through networking, your church builds relationships, captures vision for ministry opportunities, and identifies potential ministry partners.

A Relational, Asset-Based Approach

A community study with the goal of transformation does not mean academic analysis or armchair observations. It entails having a posture of serving "with" and "alongside" the community, rather than doing ministry "for" the community. Thus it is vital that the community study involve building relationships with and seeking input from members of the community. It is easy to find statistics on your community. Taking the time to be inclusive and relational will allow you to get beyond raw data to the heart of the matter.

Note that the community study takes into account the strengths and resources of the community, not just its needs and flaws. A relational, asset-based approach to community study keeps a church from having a patronizing attitude -- thinking that they (in the community) have all the problems, and we (in the church) hold all the answers. Forming relationships for the long haul also discourages the temptation to look for a "quick fix" for the community's needs.

Our understanding of common grace assures us that God is already at work in the community, that each person has God-given gifts to offer and capacities to develop, and that the church has a role in discovering and unleashing this potential. We are to build redemptive relationships that help connect members of the community to God and to one another. The value of this approach, Jay Van Groningen writes in *Communities First: Through God's Eyes, With God's Heart*, comes from "seeing all things in a community that can be used in some way to make life better for everyone" and "connecting people in wonderful exchanges of neighborly love." Think of your community study as a treasure hunt for the wheat of God's activity, hidden among the tares (Matthew 13:24-30). Begin by asking the Lord of the harvest to show you where His reign is already evident in the community. This approach will prove most fruitful as your church moves from analysis to action.

Define Your Community of Ministry

"Community of ministry" — the particular arena where the church concentrates its ministry — can mean several different things. Which of the following (from Amy Sherman, *Restorers of Hope*, pp. 23-29) best describes the way your church defines its ministry community?

- *Settlers* concentrate on the geographical neighborhoods where their churches are physically located and "work for the transformation of these neighborhoods from the inside out."
- *Gardeners* develop ministry ties with neighborhoods outside their immediate area, which they view "as extensions of their own churches (spiritual homes), in the same way that homeowners view their gardens as an extension of their houses." For example, a suburban church might "adopt" a particular inner-city neighborhood, or a church might locate a ministry in a senior center or a mall.
- *Shepherds* "primarily serve one targeted population . . . rather than a specific geographic neighborhood." A church with a commitment to persons with HIV/AIDS, low-income senior citizens, disabled persons, or Haitian immigrants, for

example, might have ministries spanning several neighborhoods.

The way you define your community of ministry should take into account existing patterns of outreach, the residential and employment patterns of the congregation, natural connections between the congregation and a community (such as ethnicity), special concerns of the congregation, and the leading of God's Spirit.

If your church is a shepherd, describe the targeted population, and the reasons for the church's relationship with this group. If your church is a settler or a gardener, identify the boundaries of the neighborhood as specifically as possible. Take note of the relationship between your ministry community and the area(s) where most church members live. Also observe significant similarities and differences (like culture or income levels) between church members and the people in the community.

Unless you already have a clearly defined ministry community, one suggestion is to settle first on a limited geographical area, then focus on a population group emerging from your study. For example, you might select your school district. From your study of this community, you may decide to focus on single parent families. Start small, while leaving room for future evolution and growth.

Check whether your church has defined different "neighbors" for different aspects of ministry — meeting social needs here while targeting evangelistic ministry there. A holistic approach ministers across the spectrum of spiritual and social needs in a community.

Methods for Learning About Your Community

Information about the community of ministry can be gathered in a variety of ways. Each of these methods can help you get to the core question for a community vision: What are one or two things that would make life better for everyone in the neighborhood?

1. **Census data and other published reports:** The census (available on the Internet, http://www.census.gov) provides a wealth of demographic information and tracks changing trends. Ask your local librarian for help in accessing the census data for your community. Other kinds of reports on your community may also be available from a local university, the school board, the chamber of commerce, or another church.

2. **Maps**: Detailed street maps can be obtained from the planning department of your municipal government. Or download a map from mapquest.com. (The Mapping Center for Evangelism and Church Growth, mappingcenter.org, is one of several Christian mapping software programs.) You can also draw your own map of your community based on your observations.

3. **Surveys**: Written or oral questionnaires ask community members to identify local needs, issues, and assets. If church members are not from the community, try to pair each member on the survey team with a local resident who knows the people in the neighborhood. While surveys can also gather information about people's background and interests, they should not be too personal or intrusive.

4. **Interviews**: Identify leaders and "insiders" in the community (elected officials, business leaders, community organizers, other pastors, long-time residents) to interview. Also includes interviews with "ordinary" members of the community. Ask about their experiences and views of the

community, their perceptions of your church, and their suggestions for how the church could impact the community's well-being.

5. **Focus groups**: Gather a group of community members to share their insights. Groups can either reflect the diversity of the community or share a common key characteristic (such as seniors, or parents of teenagers). It is helpful to start by asking broad questions about people's opinions and observations of community life — their fears and hopes, gripes and prides. As your ministry focus narrows, focus groups can target specific questions (such as what kinds of ministries for seniors are needed, or why people think so many local teens are becoming pregnant).

6. **Community informant panel**: Invite a selection of experts on the community — e.g., a school principal, city council representative, police officer, business leader, and neighborhood association representative — to a meeting at the church where each can give a brief presentation on the community and answer questions.

7. **"Insiders"**: Use church members as a resource: members who live in the community of ministry, or who work in the community, particularly in service positions such as health care providers and teachers.

8. **Observation**: Go through the community on foot ("walking surveys") or by car ("windshield surveys"). Make an effort to seek out the hidden corners, the people living on the margins. Ask a resident to give you a guided tour of the neighborhood.

9. **Participation**: Participant observation in a spirit of Christian servanthood is especially important if your community of ministry is geographically, culturally, or economically distant from your own. Suggested activities to help church members soak in community life and become more familiar with the area include:

- shopping, eating, and walking in the neighborhood.
- riding public transportation into and around the community rather than driving.
- spending an hour in the waiting room of the local emergency room, municipal court or public welfare office.
- hanging out in public spaces like parks or libraries.
- checking out community bulletin boards (often posted at places like rec centers and grocery stores);
- volunteering at a homeless shelter or other local service agency;
- attending civic, cultural, sporting, or seasonal events (town meetings, concerts, Little League games, Easter parades);
- worshiping at church services in the neighborhood.

10. **Documents**: Collect neighborhood publications, articles about the community in city newspapers, and newsletters from nonprofits that work in the community. In selecting your community assessment methods, seek a balance of qualitative and quantitative information, as the *Handbook for Urban Church Ministries* explains: You are looking for both objective and intuitive information. Intuitive insight about the neighborhood, as you can gain from conversations with residents, for example, puts living human faces on social circumstances. Objective information, as found in sources like census data, broadens individual experiences to community trends. Based on intuition alone, you might end up creating an entire program to meet needs that only one or two families are experiencing. Working with data alone, you risk simply becoming another social service agency, missing the warmth of gospel love for God's people around you.

Network with People and Institutions in the Community

Networking is the exchange of information, ideas and resources with key persons and institutions in the community. The community study and networking go hand in hand: through the community assessment process, you will discover good prospects for networking; and as you network, you will gain more insights about the community. While the information you gain from networking interviews is useful for preparing the community study report, the process of networking does not stop when the report is done. Networking is an ongoing, long term project.

The goal of networking is to build relationships, to scout out potential allies, and to let others know about your church, while gathering information about the community and ministry opportunities. Networking also builds the church's reputation as an entity that cares about the community's needs and respects others. Networking is vital to the larger goal of vision discernment and holistic ministry development.

Targets for networking include other churches (and non-Christian houses of worship); social service agencies; schools; police; social security and welfare offices; real estate agents; businesses; health clinics; foundations; and public officials. Focus on "anchor institutions" that play a key role in shaping community life and providing stability. Also become acquainted with key individuals in the community: gatekeepers, caretakers, flak-catchers, and brokers. Offer to take people out to lunch, arrange to meet for coffee, or ask for a tour of their facilities—and leave a packet of information about your church. The "Networking Interviews" tool suggests questions you can ask.

As a clearer picture emerges of the kinds of holistic ministry your church may undertake, pay special attention to potential ministry partners — programs your church could come alongside and support; sources of client referrals, volunteers or funds for your own programs; coalitions your church should join;

people who can provide special expertise; churches to team up with. Keep track of your networking contacts and any ideas for follow-up toward potential partnerships, using the "Networking Log" tool.

Another fruit of networking is the development of relationships with members of the community who can walk with your congregation as you learn about the community and lay the groundwork for outreach activities. These relationships help to build the community's trust and sense of investment in the church's ministry, while providing valuable "insider" input and access. The relationships forged through networking help to ensure that the church engages in holistic ministry *with*, not simply *to*, the community.

Whenever possible, try to link church leaders with people in the community according to their area of ministry. The youth group leader, for example, could connect with public school principals and teachers, the director of the local Boys and Girls Club, and people associated with the juvenile court system.

Community Study Guide

This guide will help you know what you are looking for as a "student of the community." Some of the questions will apply more to "community" in the sense of a geographical area; others apply more to "community" in the sense of a people group.

You can use these questions as a framework for reporting your study group's findings to the church. Feel free to add, subtract or adapt questions as appropriate to your particular context. The goal is not to answer every question, but to gather the information most relevant to your unique context and concerns.

A. <u>Look up</u>: seek God's perspective on the community

Community study should be grounded in prayer. Our ability to interpret the complex realities of the community is necessarily limited and biased. Seek the gift of seeing the community through God's eyes.

B. <u>Look around</u>: describe the community

To create a thorough portrait of a community, you have to look at it through several different "lenses."

1. Demographics: the make-up of the community. What is the current composition of the community in terms of:

   a. Total population

      b. Race, ethnicity, or language groups

      c. Age

      d. Education

      e. Employment

      f. Income

      g. Household size / family structure

• How have these characteristics changed over the last ten years?

• What trends are anticipated for the next ten years?

2. Culture: systems of meaning, values, and practices that shape how people in the community live. Consider:

   a. What do people in this community value most — family, career, homes, etc.?

b. What are the dominant religions or world views (such as individualism or humanism)? What gives people's lives meaning and hope?

c. How do people in this community like to spend their free time?

d. What unites the community, and what divides it? What are sources of tension or conflict among different groups?

3. Organization: underlying structures and systems that uphold the community's quality of life.

a. What are the major institutions that serve the area or people group (schools, businesses, churches, banks, hospitals, nonprofits, etc.)? What strengths and needs are associated with these institutions? Which institutions develop, and which drain, human resources, economic resources, and social capital?

b. What are the major systems that get important functions done (the criminal justice system, the local economy, garbage collection, public transportation, etc.)? What are the strengths and needs associated with these systems?

c. What is the condition of the physical infrastructure that sustains community life (housing stock, streets, parks, water, or waste treatment plants, etc.)?

4. Power relationships: how decisions are made that affect the community.

a. Who are the individuals and institutions who hold power in the community? Power-brokers can be both formal (ward captains) and informal (block "mamas"). Consider political power (e.g., zoning board), economic power (e.g., banks), and cultural power (e.g., media).

b. What powerful outside influences affect the quality of life in the community (neighboring municipalities, national government, business headquarters, HMOs, etc.)?

c. What are the channels of access (official and unofficial) to those in power? How much opportunity do members of the community have for input into decision-making processes?

d. Who in the community is active in challenging or influencing those in power as a response to community needs? Who speaks up on behalf of the community?

e. Who in the community has the least power? Who is most "invisible"?

5. Social capital: intangible resources for building community life.

a. Civic life: What civic organizations exist in the community to bring people together and reinforce common interests and values (e.g., amateur sports leagues, Boy/Girl Scouts, parent-teacher associations, Town Watch, block captains, book clubs)?

b. Collaborations: What networks or collaborations exist in the community that allow shared information, resources, and support (e.g., clergy coalitions, social service consortiums, leadership councils, public-private partnerships)?

c. Community identity: To what extent do people have a common community identity, a sense of belonging and attachment to one another or to the neighborhood?

      d. Community cohesion: Do people know who their neighbors are? Do people look out for one another — do they monitor the behavior of other people's kids, take pride in keeping their streets clean, alert police if they see something suspicious in their neighbor's yard?

      e. Community linkages: To what extent is the community connected with outside resources and cultural influences? Is it isolated and stagnant, or does it attract investment of outside resources and participate in the broader metropolitan area?

6. Spiritual life: spiritual realities that impact the tangible attributes of the community.

      a. What is the level of church attendance and other signs of religious commitment in the community?

      b. Does the community bear any spiritual scars from destructive events or demonic influences?

      c. What spiritual assets, such as Christian families who pray for their neighbors, uphold the fabric of community life?

      d. What are the likely sources of resistance to the gospel? What factors might contribute to openness to the gospel?

7. Geography: the location of boundaries, institutions, and special features.

      Find or create a map of your area of ministry focus. If your community is a people group, map where concentrations of these people live in your city or region, along with the key institutions that serve this community.

C. <u>Look out</u>: identify problems faced by the community

Report the problems that threaten the goodness of life in the community. There are two ways to organize this information:

in terms of people-groups, or in terms of felt needs. Choose the format that best applies to your context (or use both).

1. Needs associated with people groups

- poor persons
- elderly
- single parent households
- disadvantaged / at-risk children
- sick / disabled (and their caretakers)
- prisoners / ex-prisoners
- refugees / immigrants
- persons with addictions
- disaster victims
- other _____ (add as needed for your context)

2. Felt needs

- spiritual / moral needs (guilt, spiritual healing, emptiness, greed)
- family needs (parenting, marital problems, divorce, abuse, foster care)
- physical needs (food, shelter/housing, clothing, problems of aging)
- health needs (lack of access to quality care, disabiilties, mental health)
- emotional needs (loneliness, grief, suicide, stress, recreation)
- addictions (drugs, alcohol, sex, food, co-dependency)
- security (violent crime, property crimes, juvenile delinquency, hate crimes)

- cognitive needs (literacy, English as a second language, tutoring, drop-outs)
- employment needs (un- or under-employment, job training, living wage, day care)
- environmental needs (pollution, garbage, blight, hazards)
- sexual issues (prostitution, teenage sexuality, homosexuality)
- justice/legal concerns (legal aid, discrimination, law enforcement, political corruption)

For each major problem identified, consider:

a. How intense or widespread is this need? Where is it most concentrated?

b. What existing programs (public, private-secular, or faith-based) serve the people group or address the need? What dimensions of need remain unmet?

D. **Look back**: trace the community's history

Construct a basic timeline of the community's history.

a. What major transformations has the community undergone?

b. What happened in the past — catastrophic events, industry changes, political decisions, demographic shifts — that has a bearing on current needs?

c. What past accomplishments can the community point to with pride?

d. What key events or people may have affected the spiritual condition of the community (e.g., revivals, occult activity, church foundings/closures)

e. Who are the latest newcomers to the community, and why are they coming?

E. <u>Look within</u>: examine the church's perceptions of the community

Your preconceptions are the colored lens through which you interpret and apply information. An important step in studying your ministry context is to check the congregation's perceptions of the community.

a. How do members of the congregation describe the community? What kinds of adjectives and images do people associate with it (needy, promising, dependent, oppressed, wasteland, harvest field, danger zone)?

b. How (if at all) is the community referred to in sermons, in prayer time, in the church newsletter? Is the community on the church's radar screen?

c. What kinds of interactions has the church had with people and organizations in this community — positive, negative, indifferent? Have any conflicts arisen?

d. What kinds of natural connections exist between the church and community, such as members who live, work, own businesses or go to school there? Are these people excited about the prospect of serving the community?

F. <u>Look in the mirror</u>: see your church through the eyes of the community

"O wad some Power the giftie gie us / To see oursels as ithers see us!" (Robert Burns, "To a Louse") As you research the community, ask questions to help you see your church from the perspective of people in the community.

a. What comments do people make about the church's reputation or role in the community? (Were there any surprises?)

b. What would people like to see the church doing to help the community?

c. How welcoming and neighbor-friendly is your congregation, in terms of signage, parking, access, cleanliness, politeness, etc.?

PROCESSING THE COMMUNITY STUDY REPORT: REFLECTION QUESTIONS

Sometimes when churches do a community study, they write the report, file the report — and forget about the report. But a community study is not information for information's sake; it is gathered for the purpose of equipping the church to share the good news of the Gospel in word and deed. Keep this goal in mind. If you allow your study to get bogged down in statistics or overwhelmed with details, you will end up with "paralysis of analysis."

Use the following reflection questions to guide the analysis of the report. Dedicate time in this process to prayer. The insights yielded by this analysis, together with the ministry audit and church self-study, can then inform the larger process of discerning your church's vision for holistic mission and developing a strategic ministry plan.

1. How is God already at work in the community?

To be effective in ministry, we need to get on board with what God is already doing. A community study becomes a treasure hunt for the wheat of God's activity, hidden among the tares (Matt. 13:24-30). This approach is especially essential for distressed neighborhoods or people groups that are usually viewed in terms of their problems. Ask the Lord to show you where His reign is already evident in the community.

While we naturally gravitate toward the movers and shakers, Scripture makes it plain that God also (or even primarily) works among those at the margins. Look for the people who demonstrate God's love and build up the community through the rhythms of ordinary life, like teachers, homemakers, and sports league coaches. Identify those who have a "fire in their belly" for justice. Don't limit your search to Christians — remember that God called the idolatrous king Nebuchadnezzar "my servant" (Jer. 27:6). God can work through any person or institution to accomplish His aims.

Develop an appreciation for assets in the community. How might the church nurture a relationship with these assets and support the community development work that is already taking place? How might the church invite members of the community to share their gifts to bless one another, and to join the church in doing the work of the kingdom? Also consider the ways your church is already being used by God to bless your community.

2. What aspects of community life call for transformation by God's holy love?

Seeing brokenness around us should stir up what activist David Frenchak calls a "holy discontent." The whole creation groans under its bondage to decay, says Romans 8:21-22, and we too groan in our spirits as we yearn for Christ's complete redemption. What about the community grieves you, raises your hackles, fills you with a yearning to see things change? Who in the community is crying out for God's healing touch?

List the needs and issues that the church could respond to. Consider both the needs that are manifest in the lives of individuals (divorce, addictions, disabilities), and the problems that affect systems and institutions (immigration policies, juvenile courts, access to health care). Make sure that your responses reflect what members of the community themselves say are priority concerns, not just the needs that seem most obvious to "outsiders."

Address this question from a holistic perspective, tuning in to both spiritual and material needs. Ask the Holy Spirit to help you see the community through God's eyes, looking past the outward appearance of things to the heart of the matter (1 Samuel 16:7). In more affluent communities, we may be inclined to conclude that everything is fine. But polished exteriors can mask many forms of brokenness—family conflict, addictions, the scars of abuse, spiritual emptiness. And in low-income communities, while the eye is naturally drawn to physical evidence of need— graffiti, abandoned buildings, trash in the street—God can redirect our vision to the asset He cares about most: the people.

3. What would God's intended wholeness look like in this community?

What would God's "shalom" (peace and wholeness) look like in your community? Drawing on the extravagant stock of biblical promises, ask God what it would mean if the prayer, "Your Kingdom come," were answered in this community. This is the time for exercising the sanctified imagination, for holy dreaming. What could this community be like if people embraced God's transforming redemption, if neighbors loved one another, if the natural environment was flourishing, if social institutions treated people as responsible, valued creations made in the image of God?

This step requires caution, however. There is a fine line between dreaming of desired changes and imposing your will on others. Never assume that you know what is best for other people. Your vision must take the hopes and dreams of members of the community into account. This means building relationships with people and really listening to them.

4. How could our church participate in God's redemptive plans for the community?

Having laid out the needs, the assets, and the long-range vision, now ask: "So, what can we do about it?" Brainstorm a list of possible church responses to community issues. Include potential ministries as well as non-programmatic ideas like "making church services more appealing to the dominant culture in the community." Take special note of ministry ideas that have some grounding in things that your church, or individual church members, or people or agencies in the community are already doing. Push for ministry possibilities that are holistic — that touch people's lives spiritually, socially, and relationally, as well as seeking the good of the community on a more systemic level.

At this point, don't try to limit your ideas to what is practical or realistic. Make room for possibilities that are so big that only God could bring them about. This step is part of the process of narrowing down the options to discern a specific ministry plan.

Community Survey

*Hello, my name is .... and I'm with ....
church. We are conducting a survey of residents to help us learn more
about this community. The information will be used by our church to
plan how we can serve the neighborhood.*

Name: _____ Address: _____

Length of time lived in this community: _____
Ages of children at home: _____
Congregation (if any): _____

Local clubs, groups, or organizations your family participates in: _____ *(for example: sports league, parent-teacher association, Boy/Girl Scouts, Neighborhood Watch)*

1. What do you like best about this community? What makes this a good place to live?

_____

_____

2. What are up to three changes you'd like to see that could make life better in this community?

_____

_____

3. Our church is considering ways to bless this neighborhood. Do you have any suggestions?

4. Are you currently involved in any volunteer work, or are you interested in volunteering? Do you have specific skills or interests that you might want to contribute toward improving the community?

_____

_____

5. Is there any way we as a church can specifically pray for you?

_____

_____

6. Would you like us to follow up with you about working together to serve the community? _____

Phone: _____ Email: _____

Thank you very much for your time and information!

NETWORKING INTERVIEWS

The purpose of networking interviews is to learn from people who are knowledgeable about the community, and to make connections that can lead to fruitful ministry partnerships.

Interviewing is best done in pairs. It's helpful if one person takes notes while the other person asks the questions. Begin the interview by identifying yourself and your church. Explain the purpose for the interview (e.g., "Our church is exploring new ways of serving the community, and we're interested in learning more about the community and about your role here."). Afterwards, follow up with a thank-you note to show your appreciation for people's time.

Although the primary purpose of these visits is not evangelistic, be sensitive to the spiritual and personal concerns of those you contact. As it feels appropriate, offer to pray for or with people. Be on the lookout for hidden "family" -- brothers and sisters in Christ working for secular organizations.

The following questions are suggested for contacts with leaders of neighborhood associations, nonprofit agencies, schools, police, churches, civic clubs, or other groups. Your local government can help provide you with information concerning the most active organizations and leaders in the community. Also seek to identify and contact the "unoffcial" community leaders.

Questions for community contacts:

1. What are the greatest assets and strengths you see here? What gives you hope when you think about this community and its future?

2. What are your main concerns about life in this community? What do you see as the major social, economic, cultural, or spiritual challenges here?

3. What kinds of changes have you seen in the community? Overall, are things getting better or worse?

4. Finish the sentence: "The most important thing for people to know about this community is ..."

5. Finish the sentence: "This community will be stronger and better for everyone when ..."

6. How have you and your organization been working to improve life in the community?

7. Our church is considering ways to serve this neighborhood. Do you have any suggestions? Are there ways we might partner with your organization to serve the community?

8. Can you recommend two other people or organizations that we should talk to, to help us learn more about this community?

ABOUT THE AUTHOR

Dr. Hancock has been involved with compassion ministries for over 40 years. He began his journey while serving as a pastor and continued developing compassion ministry models while serving as a professor at New Orleans Baptist Theological Seminary. There he mobilized students to serve people in need through a variety of creative compassion ministries.

For over 20 years Dr. Hancock has served as the President and CEO of Louisiana Baptist Children's Home and Family Ministries in Monroe, Louisiana. During his tenure at the Children's Home, Dr. Hancock has expanded the work to include compassion ministries that reach 1,000s of children and families in need every year.

Dr. Hancock serves regularly as a guest speaker and preacher at conferences and in churches. His ministry theme is "Love God, Love People, Meet Needs, Share Christ."

ADDITIONAL BOOKS BY PERRY HANCOCK

The Compassionate Church:
Biblical – Missional – Transformational
Featuring the CARE Ministry Model

The Compassionate Church is a book for pastors and churches who desire to share God's love in word and deed. Dr. Hancock provides biblical and theological foundations along with practical structures and strategies for a church model that meets needs and changes lives in Jesus' name. The featured CARE Ministry Model provides a framework from which churches can develop effective compassion ministries.

Compassion Ministries For Your Church:
Opportunities to Meet Needs and Share Christ

Compassion Ministries For Your Church is a resource churches can use to develop effective ministries that meet needs and change lives. Each chapter unveils a unique ministry carefully selected for its potential to resonate with diverse congregations and address a variety of pressing needs found in almost every community. Practical, actionable steps are also provided to help churches initiate and sustain each ministry. In addition, two detailed assessment instruments are included. *Compassion Ministries For Your Church can help your church reach your community by sharing God's love in word and deed.*

Created For Good Works:
Encouraging the Church to Serve

According to Ephesians 2:10, believers are created in Christ Jesus to do the good works of God. The church has been called to serve. *Created For Good Works* is a compilation of conference presentations, sermons, and lectures on Christian service that the author has made over the past three decades. Excerpts from two other books by the author are also included. The goal is simple - That the followers of Christ through His church will meet needs, share the good news of the Savior, and change the world in Jesus' name. Welcome to *Created For Good Works*.

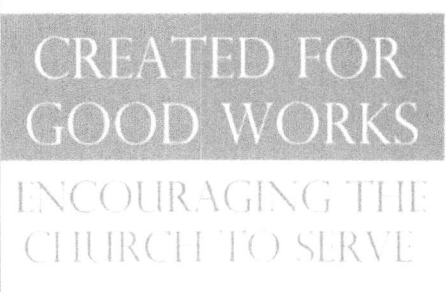

Changing Hearts – Saving Lives:
Rescuing the Poor in Jesus' Name

Changing Hearts Saving Lives is a book that takes you on a journey of personal reflection and decision regarding one of the most challenging issues of our day - Poverty. Dr. Hancock begins by sharing his own childhood experience with poverty. He continues by asserting that caring and kindness are not enough to make a lasting difference in the lives of the poor. More must be done. This book challenges Christians and the church to embark upon a rescue mission that could change the world.

My Field of Roses (*A Christian Novel*)

Steven and Sarah have lost their mother, Anne. She was only fifty-five years old, and she was the most important person in their lives. Two weeks before her death, Anne gave Sarah a small box filled with family photos and other memorabilia. While going through the items, Steven and Sarah discover an unusual mystery from the past that must be solved. The two travel to rural Mississippi searching for answers but find more questions about their mother's heritage. Their search eventually leads to the discovery of an incredible family secret that Anne had kept hidden for decades. When the truth is revealed, Steven and Sarah are amazed at their mother's courage and strength.

Made in United States
Orlando, FL
14 April 2025